CAR BUYING, HER WAY

THE FIERCE GIRL'S ROADMAP TO THE CAR OF YOUR DREAMS

LISA C. COPELAND

FINN-PHYLLIS PRESS

PRAISE FOR CAR BUYING, HER WAY

"Lisa Copeland is highly respected within her industry as THE authority when it comes to encouraging and supporting women within the automotive space. Even more importantly, Lisa is treasured by all the women she has mentored, inspired, encouraged, hired, and promoted within this male-dominated industry. She is a champion for the industry and a role model for all women looking to excel in it."

—Sharon Lechter, author of Think and Grow Rich for Women, co-author of Outwitting the Devil, Three Feet From Gold, New York Times bestseller Rich Dad Poor Dad, and 14 other books in the Rich Dad series.

"Lisa Copeland is the real deal. Her experience and high level of success when it comes to women's issues in the car dealership world is unique and inspiring. I hold Lisa in the highest regard and endorse her mission: empowering women when it comes to car buying at dealerships, supporting and mentoring women's careers, and growing more female leaders in the automotive industry."

—Jody DeVere, co-founder, Women in Automotive LLC and CEO, AskPatty.com, Inc.

"Lisa Copeland's enthusiasm for life and compassion for others is evident from the first page to the last. Women are either involved in or the sole decision maker in over 70 percent of automotive purchases, and Lisa identifies the unique male/female purchasing differences as well as how to prepare yourself or your team to deliver!"

—*Adam Arens, Owner, Patriot Automotive Group*

"With women being the number one influencer in the car buying process, it's critical that both they and the dealerships anxious to serve them to be prepared for a Car Buying, Her Way experience. Lisa Copeland does a phenomenal job of preparing consumers and dealers for getting a fantastic deal; having an incredible experience; and retaining long-term, satisfied customers."

—*Dan Moore, President, Vistadash*

Published by Finn-Phyllis Press, Inc.

Car Buying, Her Way / Lisa C. Copeland - 1st ed.

ISBN 978-1-7330337-2-5 (eBook)

ISBN 978-1-7330337-3-2 (pbk)

www.LisaCopeland.com

To all of the consumers and everyone else who has taken this journey with me.

FOREWORD

BY CHRIS MARTINEZ

I still remember the first time I walked into a dealership to buy a vehicle. It wasn't the best experience, to say the least. I remember feeling very uncomfortable—I instantly felt uneducated and aware that I needed to know far more than I did. I was twenty years old and remember a kind female sales consultant bringing me a piece of paper with nothing on it, simply saying, "Sign here." I was presented with all kinds of numbers I didn't understand. I remember the sense that she too felt uncomfortable as she approached her manager, who sat behind a glass wall. I also remember the look on his face when I didn't sign the paper. They wouldn't take me to the next step before I signed. I ended up walking out, thinking, "Wow, that was scary." I couldn't believe that they were trying to push me into purchasing a car without driving it or receiving any real explanation about what I was purchasing. As a result, I saved my money and bought a vehicle from a private party just so I wouldn't have to have that experience again.

Fast-forward a few years to the day I bought a new phone case to put on my buckle (yes, it was a while ago). A friend of mine said,"Man, you look like a car salesman." I was instantly offended. A year later, a car dealership was recruiting my brother. He wasn't interested in the position at that time; he was successful and happy where he was professionally. It was a new company, and I decided that if they wanted my twin brother, I was the next best thing. So, I went in his place. I didn't realize at the time that it was a car dealership because my brother told me it was Carmex—like the lip balm—and the interview was held at a hotel.

Despite my initial confusion, I was impressed with the organization and the way they greeted me and were treating candidates. Once they further explained who and what they were, I was sold (pun intended). I instantly believed that I could do things differently from the way I was treated when I tried to buy a car for the first time. My goal was simple: I was going to treat people properly, the way I wished I'd been treated.

I've been in the car business for over sixteen years, and have both been a part of companies that have scaled very fast and companies I've helped take to the next level. As a father of four (including three girls), I've always done my part to take extra good care of the women who come in to purchase a vehicle. My hope is that when my daughters are on their own, salespeople with the same approach I've taken will take care of them.

I've known Lisa Copeland for several years. I initially knew of her based on her reputation as a car dealer. She was a part-owner of the number one FIAT dealership in the country, which was—at the time—located in a well-known mall in Austin, Texas called The Domain. What was fascinating about the location was that it was in a mall, and a car dealership selling over one hundred cars out of it was an incredible feat. The way she was able to build her community and the loyalty of her customers out of such a tiny space was truly remarkable. Her drive and go-getter personality have netted her a well-respected following in automotive, but her caring nature and community involvement have built her reputation with clients all over the US.

As a board member of Woman in Automotive, Lisa has a reputation for being able to cater to female buyers in a remarkable way. She's built her company, Cars Her Way, into the only marketing company in the country that caters to the needs of the female car buyer. Her approach and process have given her a strong voice in the automotive space, and as her friend and business partner, I truly admire her tenacious attitude and drive.

This book will provide any buyer with the tools to enter a car dealership with confidence and the ability to negotiate a fair deal while navigating the process of purchasing a vehicle. Car buying doesn't have to be difficult, a fact that Lisa articulates phenomenally through this book. Put simply, *Cars Her Way* is a must-read for anyone who wishes to walk into a dealership armed with everything you need to have a successful transaction, purchase the car of your dreams, and hopefully have a little fun along the way. The automotive industry is a great one that affords many opportunities—not based on education or skill set but on a love of connecting with and serving people. Who knows? By the end, you may want to enter the automotive business yourself!

INTRODUCTION

And one day she discovered that she was fierce and strong and full of fire, and that not even she could hold herself back because her passion burned brighter than her fears.
—Mark Antony

Even I don't like to go to a dealership to buy a car, and I owned an incredibly successful dealership! In March 2016, I sold my award-winning dealership in Austin, Texas. I quickly went from owning 800 cars to owning zero cars. I decided after I sold the store that I wanted to buy a new Mercedes SUV, so I did what every other consumer does: I got online, read the reviews, looked at available inventory around town, and chose my car.

After I identified the car I wanted to purchase, I said to my husband, "Why don't you go down there and work the deal; I'll come pick it up at the time of delivery." When I later showed up at the delivery, everybody was gobsmacked that I had not gone down there myself to work the deal. After all, wasn't I all about empowering female consumers—especially in this industry?

I said, "Guys, this activity is not a fun one for me." I wanted to be involved in only the best part, which was picking up my new car. That was a very important moment for me, and the one in which I knew beyond a shadow of a doubt that Cars Her Way needed to be birthed. I answer hundreds of emails, texts, and Facebook messages every single month from women (and men) all over the country who are in the process of looking at or buying a car, and the top questions I receive are, "Lisa, is this a good deal?" "Lisa, should I try to drive the car first?" and "Lisa, what do you recommend?"

My dear friend and mentor, *New York Times* bestselling author Sharon Lechter, told me a long time ago that you have a business if you can solve a problem and serve a need. *Cars Her Way* was created to do both of those things. I wanted to create a space through a website, radio show, book, and network of highly vetted, trusted dealer partners that would provide predominantly female consumers (as well as the businesses that serve them) with my thirty years of knowledge as well as a community where they could come together to share the best practices of the best car dealers in the nation. I'm all about the practice of buying a new car as often as you want one, and this is my way of pressuring the entire industry to level up, to create an experience for the number one influencer in the world: women.

I have shopped by committee for years. When I need to go out and look for the perfect dress for an occasion, I *never* go alone. I call my posse because I don't trust my own judgment. Consumer trends show that I'm not alone in that approach. Many direct sales companies in the clothing industry such as Cabi have flourished based on the business model of "party plan" clothing buying. The premise is to bring women together and allow them to shop in the comfort of their own home while enjoying the experience of trying on the latest fashions in front of their tribe before buying their seasonal wardrobe by committee.

Hey automotive industry, news flash: women love to shop! So, why is there such a large disparity between loving to shop and completing a car purchase? Imagine having a "party plan" network marketing company that sold cars. Now there's a concept!

The auto industry is one of the most important industries in the United States, historically contributing three to three-and-a-half percent to the overall Gross Domestic Product. I want to share with you some really important stats.

- The purchasing power of women in the US ranges from $5 trillion to $15 trillion annually. (Source: Nielsen Consumer, 2013)
- Women control more than 60% of all personal wealth in the US (Source: Federal Reserve, MassMutual Financial Group, BusinessWeek, Gallup)
- Women purchase over 50% of traditional male products, including automobiles, home improvement products, and consumer electronics. (Source: Andrea Learned, "Don't Think Pink")
- Approximately 40% of US working women now out-earn their husbands. (Source: U.S Bureau of Labor Statistics)
- Women influence 85% of all purchases. That includes healthcare, automotive, and education.

- Women are responsible for $7 trillion in U.S Consumer spending.
- Two-thirds of all consumer wealth will belong to women in the next decade
- Fifty percent of the products marketed to men are bought by women. Wow.
- 74.9% of women identified themselves as the primary shoppers for their households (Source: GFK MRI, Survey of the American Consumer, 2011)
- 61% of women are more likely to include an item on their list if they're currently using the brand, 57% if they have a coupon, or 56% if they have seen the item in a store ad or circular. (Source: Integer Group and M/A/R/C Research, 2012)
- 92% of women pass along information about deals or online recommendations to others. (Source: Mindshare/Ogilvy & Mather)
- In 61% of all consumer electronics purchases, a woman either initiated the purchase or was involved in the purchase process. (Source: Consumer Electronics Association (2012)

And, drum roll please...women spend *$2 billion* on new cars and mechanical servicing of vehicles in the US every year.[1] They should be able to have a confident, enjoyable experience purchasing those cars!

Therefore, this book is intended to provide everything you need as an automotive consumer so you'll have all of your questions answered ahead of time. Think about it—every great athlete has a coach and an agent. When you buy a new home, you likely don't try to do so all by yourself. You partner with a real estate agent. You work with a title company and an attorney to look over the documents. Why in the world would you go to the car dealership without a similar kind of coach and agent? I'm here to be your coach, agent, *and* cheerleader. I want to help you negotiate the best deal you can—one that's fair both to you and to the automotive retailer you're doing business with. They have a right to make money, but they don't need to make it all off of you and you alone! By the time you finish reading this book, you will have all the knowledge you need to negotiate your next car deal so that you can drive away in the car of your dreams.

In addition to coaching you through the purchase of your dream car, I want to share with you many of the business lessons and insights I've gleaned over the years while reaching for great success in this industry. These Fierce Girl Business tips, hacks, and insights that can benefit you no matter the industry you're in, whether it's male-dominated or not. Shortcuts to having the business of your dreams combined with shortcuts that will allow you to drive to that business every day in the car of your dreams sounds like a great partnership!

I created the FIERCE brand as an acronym to remind myself that, in order to achieve the goals I have in life, I must commit to be Unapologetically FIERCE 365 days a year.

Fearless
Initiative
Enthusiastic
Relentless
Crush Approval Addition
Execute

As you'll learn, there is FIERCE in everything I undertake. So let's get to it.

1

NECESSITY BREEDS GREATNESS

"A strong woman looks a challenge in the eye and gives it a wink."
—*Gina Carey*

People frequently ask me, "How did you get into the car business, Lisa?" Or "How did you and James meet thirty-five years ago?" Both happened by accident (literally). Sometimes, life takes you down unexpected roads. Mine certainly did. In fact, one specific, fateful day changed the entire trajectory of my life and career.

In 1984, I was a 19-year-old fashion major in Dallas, Texas, happily selling skirts for three dollars an hour plus commissions at Contempo Casuals in The Galleria mall in Dallas. One day while driving to work, late as usual, I was doing my version of multitasking—you know, driving while applying my makeup—when all of a sudden...*crash*! I had rear-ended a gentlemen who was driving a big van on Webbs Chapel Rd.

I jumped out of the car and ran up to his van yelling,

"Why did you hit the brakes?" He was just as angry as I was, and started screaming back at me. I was so upset. There weren't yet cell phones, so in order to call my parents, I walked up to the house on the corner of Webbs Chapel and Camelot and knocked on the door. A nice young man answered, and by that time I was hysterical. I knew my car was wrecked, I had this man screaming at me, and I was late for work. James Copeland introduced himself to me, invited me in, and pulled out his Yellow Pages phone book so he could call my boss and tell her what had happened. He then proceeded to go outside and get all the insurance info from the angry man, who turned out to be his neighbor. Cooler heads prevailed, thank God.

The next day, I took my car to the body shop, and they proceeded to tell me that the front end was totalled. I was so naive that I wasn't even quite sure what that meant. After all, I'd driven the car to the body shop, so how could it be totalled? The manager said, "You need to call your insurance company and file a claim." I still remember the knot I felt in my stomach when he I needed to call my insurance company.

I called them and said, "I wrecked my car. What do I need to do next?" After pulling up my account, the gal on the other end of the line said, "Well, it would help if you paid your insurance premiums." Of course I argued with her, declaring that I mailed my checks; they must have gotten lost. She wasn't buying that and proceeded to tell me that my insurance had been cancelled six months prior; there was nothing they could do to reinstate it. I was terrified. What was I going to do? My parents had sent me a monthly allowance, part of which was to cover my car expenses. I rationalized that at least I had paid my rent, which was a good thing given that living in my car was no longer an option!

As would any determined fashion major, I was spending all of my money on clothes and shoes. I knew that purchasing a new car would be incredibly tough, but I had no other option. I didn't have a down payment or a credit score, so I had no choice but to call my parents (who lived in California) and fess up about what had happened to my beautiful 1982 green Chevy Cutlass Supreme.

When my dad answered the phone, the conversation went something like this:

"Dad, I was driving to work, and this dumb man in front of me slammed on his brakes and, well, I rear ended him. It was *all* his fault, Dad, and I was even late to work so my boss was mad at me."

My dad asked if I was okay and then said, "Don't worry, that's what insurance is for. Have you called your insurance company yet?" I burst into tears and told him that I called, but they said that my insurance had been cancelled for non-payment. He was *furious* with me. I went on to tell him that I'd met a nice guy who was a car salesman. In fact, I'd knocked on his door just after the accident. He could sell me a new Camaro, and my dad would just need to co-sign.

"Co-sign?" my dad responded, sounding horrified. "That Cutlass was paid for, and no, I am not co-signing, giving you any portion of the down payment, or subsidizing your monthly payment." What he said next defined my life from that point forward:

"You need to figure it out, kid."

Figure it out? There was nothing to figure out! I needed a car. Dallas did not have a very good public transportation system, and Uber was non existent. What was I going to do?

Remember James? The nice young man who helped me during my Damsel in Distress moment after wrecking my car? He had gotten my phone number (rather, the number of the pay phone in the dorm) and came to see me a few times when I was working at the mall. One day, after telling him about my woes, he suggested that I get a job selling cars. He had just graduated from college and taken a job at a local Chevy store, and he loved it. He told me all about the perks, the income potential, *and* his brand new Chevy Celebrity demo. I said, "That's great for you, but you're a guy. Girls don't sell cars."

"Yes they do!" he replied. "We have one, and she does really well." I had never even set foot in a car dealership, and the highest ticket item I had ever sold was a $29 skirt. Also, what did I know about cars? Absolutely nothing. The idea of selling them seemed as impossible as did raising the money for a down payment or finding a co-signer. I felt quite defeated and *really* scared. What was I going to do? James told me he had a friend and former officemate named Ernie who had just left his store and started at a rival Chevy dealership across town. He would call him and see if we could have lunch.

James, Ernie, and I had lunch the next week. Ernie was sixty years old and an automotive veteran. He was lovely and kind. He said, "Any friend of James is a friend of mine. Let me see what I can do to get you an interview with my managers." That ended up being far easier said than done. None of the managers at Jim Johnson Chevrolet were interested in a nineteen-year-old fashion major. I had never seen or heard so much rejection. They seemingly said and did everything possible to discourage me from working at their dealership. It was a boys club, and they weren't interested in training a teenaged girl to sell cars.

Within one particular interview, the sales manager said,

"This business is for men. You don't belong here. You don't have what it takes." Another manager said, "Selling skirts is what women do; selling cars is what men do. We are not interested."

Completely discouraged, I arranged to have a second lunch with my new friend, Ernie. I thanked him for his help securing interviews for me, and described the kinds of responses I received from the dealership's management team. He told me that he had one more trick up his sleeve and asked me to meet him again the following day. The next day, I met him at Jim's Restaurant in Plano, and Ernie said, "You're in. I went to the big boss and told him I was going to personally train you. I said they could put you in my office, and I will show you the ropes. Now, you're going to have to do as I say and follow directions, but I will help you. You start tomorrow."

I couldn't believe it. Ernie was my guardian angel as was, of course, James, who had introduced the two of us. As of the publishing of this book, Ernie is alive and well at ninety-two years old, and we're still in touch. I am so grateful that he was willing to help me and teach me. As for James Copeland, the nice young man who made all this happen? We have been married for thirty years and have two wonderful children and two grandchildren. The day I wrecked my (uninsured) car still stands out so vividly in my mind. I met my future husband *and* discovered an unexpected career that I've come to love so much...all by accident!

My first months working at the dealership were rocky, but Ernie truly helped me navigate the rough waters. I showed up on Day One and was given the keys to my brand new Chevy Celebrity demo. I was pumped! I had no idea the roads that lay ahead for me in the automotive industry: the good, the great, and the ugly. So keep reading because it gets better! It is extremely challenging for women to work in (not to mention be successful in) a male-dominated industry. I think about the times I would have left, and there were thousands of those times. But I also knew that if I left, I would lose the demo car I was provided.

I learned a lot of life lessons while selling cars at that car dealership, and I had a lot of success—not because I was the best closer or the best salesperson, but because I truly cared about people. I cared about people more than I cared about the process or even making the sale sometimes. That approach didn't always bode well with my boss, but it did with my clients. And on that approach, I spent the next thirty years building a very successful automotive sales career in Dallas, Texas that I'm extremely proud of. It wasn't easy, and it took its toll on a few levels. There were long hours, horrible bosses, and bad cultures to suffer through. If you can imagine it, I likely lived it. It wasn't until I had the opportunity to be part of the re-launch of the FIAT/Alfa Romeo brand in the US that I finally saw the true light—an opportunity to turn the automotive industry upside down. Not only was it a re-launch for this particular car brand, it was a personal brand relaunch.

In 2010, I was consulting as a sales strategist on a project for a central Texas Chrysler dealer. He was invited to Detroit to see what Chrysler had planned for the relaunch of FIAT in the US. It's important to note that, at this time, the automotive industry was at an all-time low. It was essentially operating in a coma, especially the Chrysler dealers. The bankruptcies, government bailouts, and factory-ordered store closings were top of mind when those Chrysler dealers hit Detroit for the FIAT meetings.

I remember when a young Chrysler executive named

Justin Byrd hit the stage. Justin was in his mid-thirties, handsome, and well spoken. He had a different vibe from any other factory executive I had met, and he had a really tough sell on his hands. His mission was to convince a room full of weary dealers that they needed to—one more time—invest in the Chrysler Corporation. That they needed to build buildings, invest in renovations, hire staff, and welcome this new product line to their communities. There was only one problem: the brand he was asking everyone to invest in was FIAT, which had gained a reputation as Fix It Again Tony!

Allow me to set the stage of the room's demeanor that day. We had all flown in to Detroit in blizzard conditions and were escorted to Chrysler World Headquarters. At that time, Detroit was a bit of a ghost town, both inside the building and on the city streets. Dealers were weary, frustrated, mad, you name it. And then there was me. I had no real skin in the game; I was simply an automotive sales strategist there on assignment. I was so excited to wander the same halls as one of my personal heroes, Lee Iacocca. Although weary, I knew that we were standing on the shoulders of greatness.

As we entered the meeting hall, I noticed the beautiful art: car hoods and fenders beautifully painted with artistic, edgy street and tattoo designs. None of us truly knew the full extent of why we were there, but we showed up anyway. Out walked high-energy, handsome Justin, who greeted us and then said something that made me sit straight up in my chair.

He said, "When was the last time you did something for the first time?"

Wow, when WAS the last time? I wondered to myself. Justin had me at *Hello,* and after he finished speaking, he introduced the woman who would be the head of the FIAT brand: Laura Soave. She was just as fabulous as Justin, and her energy and enthusiasm for the brand was contagious, at least in my eyes. They issued a challenge to everyone in that room: "You have a blank slate to launch this brand. As such, you must submit to us renderings for your facility, sales and marketing strategies, hiring strategies, and launch strategies." To work we went. It was a group project, but sales strategy and location were my pieces to figure out.

We put a lot of thought into our proposed facility. After coming back home to Austin and driving around to look for potential "traditional" dealership facilities, I drove to a shopping center called The Domain. The Domain is a high-density office, retail, and residential center, and I didn't really think anything there would be big enough or available. And then I drove up to a 6,000-square-foot, empty corner shell in the shopping centre. It was perfect. It had parking in front (which wasn't common at this location), an attached parking garage in the back (which would be a great place to store some cars and provide additional customer parking), and a large "display" pad out front on which I could showcase a car. It was a very lucky and rare find. And to think that after we moved out several years later, it became The Pretty Kitty, a waxing establishment...

We hired an architect, and the magic began. The idea of bringing the cars to the people made so much sense. At that time, The Domain was the only shopping center in Austin that also included residential living. It is a magical place that combines outdoor shopping at retailers such as Apple, Tiffany's, and Neiman Marcus with hundreds of residences. I truly believed these were our people—an entire community of early adopters and people who wanted the "city life." That is what I believed the FIAT was: the car for the early adopters and lifestyle enthusiasts. No one knew for sure how well it would (or wouldn't) be received, but the bet paid off in spades, and that 6,000-square-foot facility was the number FIAT retailer in North America for many years.

I created a sales strategy that included a finale-style delivery of the cars and decided that we would focus on hiring young millennials, women, and minorities for our sales team. I wasn't interested in hiring people who had been in the space for a long time, referred to in the industry as "retreads." Truth be told, they weren't interested in the FIAT brand anyway. I was truly inspired, and decided it was my time to leave my thumbprint on the automotive industry. I also quickly learned that when you go against the status quo, most won't join or support you. It didn't take long for me to discover who were my friends and who were my foes. Just a sampling of the pushback I heard from both friends and family included:

"Nobody in Texas buys tiny cars."

"That's an Italian rust bucket; I had one in college."

"You've never been a general manager; you're going to fail."

"A shopping mall? Seriously?"

"Stick to what you know. Relaunching a failed brand is not in your wheelhouse."

"A showroom full of female car salespeople and millenials? Have you lost your mind?"

Hopefully, you get the picture. Full of excitement as well as *tons* of self doubt, I proceeded to invest my life savings in a product that I believed would revolutionize the auto industry.

In 2011, I became the managing partner and general manager of FIAT/Alfa Romeo of Austin. And what a ride it was. I learned a lot, sacrificed a lot, and believed even more, and I wouldn't trade any of it for the world. I *loved* that little car and all that it stood for. The leadership at FIAT USA was second-to-none, and I am forever grateful for the support they offered me, both personally and professionally. One person in particular I want to acknowledge is Brent Rayfield. Brent was my Number Two from Day One. It wasn't easy, but he always rose to the occasion. He stood by me day-in and day-out, and he fought to make every deal happen. I am forever grateful for all the years he served as my co-captain.

Being part of FIAT's re-emergence to the US gave me the opportunity to be a small piece of a change in the automotive industry that greatly needed to happen (and continue to evolve). I wanted to create something aspirational while showing what had been—and still is—a predominantly male-dominated industry that female leaders and consumers are more valuable than they ever imagined. In order to accomplish this, I decided that we would do things differently, and that started with taking the risk to open a boutique dealership in a high-end shopping center.

Ironically, pieces of my fashion roots kept rearing their beautiful head throughout my automotive career. One of my earliest decisions was that we should build a $30,000 runway down the middle of our showroom floor so that we could give clients the finale delivery that they deserved. Let me tell you, car runways do *not* exist. We hired a local architect and brought him to the space. I laid out my vision, and told him that the runway needed to hold at least three cars for display and have a turntable at the end so the cars could be photographed from every angle during delivery. It needed to be strong enough to hold all those cars. I wanted it to be white and have lights on it. My vision was then built, and it served its purpose beautifully.

So, why was I intent on providing customers with a finale-style delivery? Because the delivery of the car is oftentimes the *worst* experience for a consumer. They have spent four to eight hours haggling back and forth, and by the time the car is delivered, they are ready to get the hell out of that dealership! I had a completely different lens when it came to what we called the finale. After all, the finale is the best part of the fashion show. It's when all the beautiful models and designers walk the runway and everybody celebrates that season's line. Why should the purchase of a car be any different? Why should people not celebrate making what is likely the second largest purchase of their life? We set up chairs around the stage and had customers invite their friends to celebrate right along with them. Deliveries were scheduled, and a customer's new car was placed on the runway shielded with a car cover, only to be revealed when everyone had arrived. One of my staff members (usually Matt Rheinhart) then drove that beautiful car off the runway and into the arms (metaphorically speaking) of its new owners. FIAT customers were truly the coolest ever. They named their cars, usually choosing something italian and exotic, and they truly had a love affair with them. That just doesn't happen at the Chevy store!

FIERCE Girl's Car Buying Hack

Even though the delivery event we gave our customers may seem over the top, and I don't know another dealer in the USA who has a runway down the middle of their showroom, you should still look forward to the delivery of your brand-new car. I recommend that you schedule the delivery so that you have the time to be able to enjoy it and to work with your salesperson or delivery specialist to make sure that you understand all the bells and whistles of your new car. Perhaps bring a friend along, snap some pictures, and celebrate! I have found that when I rush anything—especially such a large purchase—it goes from excitement to full-blown anxiety. Don't let the dealership rush you into taking delivery the same day if you would prefer to come back at another scheduled time. My customers constantly told me that watching that new car come down the runway was such a memorable experience, and that it made them feel confident that they had made a good decision. I hear way too many horror stories (from both women *and* men) who felt crammed into their purchase and shoved out the door. That is NOT Cars Her Way!

When people purchase a new home, they often have housewarming parties where all their friends come over and see their new home. Why was a large purchase not celebrated in the same way in the automotive industry? It didn't matter—that's the way it *was* celebrated at my dealership. We looked at the automotive industry a different way, treated our customers like they were our friends, and celebrated with them this important milestone in their life—the purchase of a new car!

One of my proudest moments was in 2012, when my young sales team broke the world sales record for the FIAT brand. In fact, the backstory to the record-breaking sale made international news. In March 2012, I was on a month-end phone call with Tim Kuniskis, who was, at the time, the head of the FIAT brand. We were reviewing the month-end numbers and discussing sales strategy for both my store and the brand as a whole. I had asked Tim many times if he would introduce me to Sergio Marchionne, who was then the CEO of both FCA and the FIAT USA/Ferrari brand. Mr. Marchionne was a personal hero of mine, and meeting him was definitely on my bucket list. Tim proceeded to let me know that such a meeting was not happening. Mr. Marchionne was the CEO of FIAT globally, head of the Europeon auto union, and CEO of Ferrari and FCA. Needless to say, he was a bit busy.

But I was relentless.

I somehow talked Tim into making a bet that would change both my life and the trajectory of my career. The bet he suggested was simple, but far from easy: we had to break the NAFTA (North American Free Trade Agreement) record for the most FIAT 500s hatchbacks sold in one month, which was 100. Beating that sales number was a tall order in 2012. FIAT only had one model at the time, we were the number one retailer in the nation, and yet the highest number we'd sold in one month up to that point was seventy. So we had to find a way to lift by thirty percent in order to hit the goal.

Tim took the bet.

I was determined to meet Sergio. My team fell short the first month—by nine cars—and I somehow convinced Tim to extend the bet by one month. In April 2012, my team not only hit the goal but surpassed it by nine units. 109 FIAT 500s sold in a single month out of a boutique showroom living amongst truck and SUV dealerships.

Tim agreed to the bet to begin with because he didn't think it could become a reality. He didn't doubt my team's abilities, but he had a line of sight to our inventory, and he knew we didn't have enough cars in stock to hit the target sales numbers. In fact, he warned me about that when we extended the bet. I assured him that if he would agree to extend the bet, I would source necessary inventory from other dealers. He also admitted to me after I won the bet that he had not told Mr. Marchionne about it. Let me tell you, it was one great sales close when I was able to call Tim and tell him to tell Mr. Marchionne to gas up the G5. He was coming to Texas.

Tim tried every approach he could think of to "modify" the bet so he wouldn't have to admit to the most powerful man in the automotive industry that he had made a bet on his behalf...and lost. One of his offers was dinner with George Clooney, as he was a FIAT Italian spokesperson. I always knew that meeting Mr. Marchionne would change my life, but imagine telling my husband, "Hey babe, I am having dinner in Italy with George Clooney." Now *that* would have been life-changing! In all seriousness, however, I had zero interest in meeting George Clooney. I told Tim, "Absolutely no Clooney." Only Sergio would do.

Both Tim and Marchionne held up Tim's end of the bet. In June 2012, Mr. Sergio Marchionne arrived at my dealership along with a full motorcade and the international press corps. We had a private meeting prior to the press conference. When he walked into the room, I jumped out of my chair. He grabbed my hands, looked me in the eyes, and said, "You choose me over George Clooney?"

Needless to say, the meeting was the absolute highlight of my automotive career. During the meeting, Sergio asked, "Is there anything else I can do for you?" I told him I would love to have my own one-of-a-kind hot pink FIAT 500 Abarth. So, he commissioned it to be built, fully custom from the paint to the interior. It was the only one like it in the world, and it was given the VIN 001. Mr. Marchionne passed away in February 2018 after a short illness. To say I was devastated is an understatement. He was a visionary, a genius, and truly one of the kindest people I have ever met. He made me believe that *anything* is possible if you believe and are willing to do the work. I am forever grateful to him and his global leadership of FCA.

The years I spent running the FIAT dealership confirmed for me that buying a car doesn't need to be a painful or an intimidating experience. Let's dive in, so I can explain a bit more about the industry as it pertains to women and show you exactly how to buy your first or next car and steer clear of both common and lesser-known landmines in the process. While it is my hope that every dealer in the country will read this book in order to gain insights into how best to attract, serve, and retain their female customers, my most important goal is to take care of the consumers who have always taken care of me.

FIERCE Girl's Business Tip

May I divert from car buying for a moment? I'd like to share with you the personal lessons I learned from making this bet with Tim. First and foremost, absolutely *nothing* is out of reach if we set our minds to it. I proved to an industry that even the little guys (or, in this case, girls) can win big. FIAT was and is the smallest brand within the FCA family as well as the automotive industry as a whole. I showed myself and my team that making a very risky and audacious bet can pay off. As I look back, I recognize that even if we hadn't broken the record, I was capable of branching out of my comfort zone and taking a chance. That at 45 years old, I still had a hell of a lot to offer, both personally and professionally.

I hope that what you take away from this chapter is not that I was the world's greatest saleswoman but that I left it all on the field. I hope to encourage just one reader—male or female—to do the same. You will never accomplish that which you don't try to accomplish. As Michael Jordan said, "You will miss 100 percent of the shots you don't take." So take the shot! If I can do it, so can you. I encourage you to commit to being unapologetically FIERCE 365 days a year! Think about it in these terms: Who is the one person who, if you met them, could change your life or career? What are you willing to do to meet them? (No restraining orders, please.) Who is your Sergio?

Disruptive trends that will transform the automotive industry

There are changing beliefs when it comes to consumer behaviors that are important to understand.[2] Doing so will only increase your confidence as you approach a stereotypically intimidating purchasing experience.

I read an interesting article a few months ago that stated that today's teenagers are no longer racing to the DMV to get a driver's license. I don't know about the rest of you, but I was at the DMV on the very day I turned sixteen, as were both of my children. That day marked a rite of passage and a newfound freedom. It was our first step into adulthood.

When I arrived at the DMV on my sixteenth birthday, I was beyond ready. I got behind the wheel and proceeded to *completely fail* the parallel parking test. I was devastated when I got back to school—I hadn't driven there myself as I'd planned but was instead dropped off by my aunt. On my daughter, Allix's sixteenth birthday, I had a cake made with a picture of her Texas drivers license on it, which I brought to school to celebrate! She was a bit mortified to see herself on a nine-by-twelve-inch cake, but you get the point: it was a time to celebrate.

We're already seeing early signs that the importance of car ownership is declining. In the United States, for example, the share of young people (ages sixteen to twenty-four) who hold a driver's license dropped from 76 percent in 2000 to 71 percent in 2013, while there has simultaneously been a greater than 30 percent annual growth in car-sharing members in North America as well as Germany over the last five years.

Reasons to support this decline include the high cost of insurance for teen drivers (premiums average $300 per month), rideshare availability through services such as Uber and Lyft, parental fear of distracted driving/texting, and the availability of car sharing apps and subscription-based programs.

The subscription-based model is one I am very familiar with. In 2015, the first subscription-based transportation solution approached me at my dealership and asked us to pilot their program. The company, flexdrive, was truly ahead of its time when it came to mobility solutions.

They dropped 120 cars at my dealership, brought in a team, and we were in business. Imagine, you could "subscribe" weekly to whatever car you needed at that time. That weekly subscription fee covered the mileage, repairs, insurance, and everything else you needed. The only contribution a subscriber needed to cover was gas. One week, someone might need a small city car, the next week she might need a truck, and the following week perhaps she'd need an SUV. There was no long-term commitment; all one needed to participate was a valid driver's license and a credit card. We found a sweet spot with Uber drivers, millennials and folks visiting from out of town since the subscription-based model was less expensive than a car rental.

The fact of the matter is, traditional consumers are aging out of driving, and new consumers have different ideas about transportation. In fact, one out of every ten cars sold in 2030 is projected to potentially be a shared vehicle.

We also continue to hear about autonomous vehicles, but what does that really mean? According to McKinsey and Company, fully autonomous vehicles are unlikely to be commercially available before 2020. However, once technological and regulatory issues have been resolved, up to 15 percent of new cars sold in 2030 could be fully autonomous. Meanwhile, Advanced Driver Assistance Systems (ADAS) will play a crucial role in preparing regulators, consumers, and corporations for the medium-term reality of cars taking over control from drivers.

Consumers today use their cars as all-purpose vehicles, whether they are commuting by themselves to work or taking the whole family to the beach. In the future, they may want the flexibility to choose the best solution for a specific purpose—on demand and via their smartphones.

All this to say, I believe that the dealership face of the retail automotive industry is changing as rapidly as is our tendency to switch smartphones. I believe that, before long, automotive dealers will have full transportation solutions available at their dealerships, offering everything from subscription-based to ride share services, and the really innovative dealerships will look into scooters and maybe even bicycles. The way people want to get from point A to point B has shifted, especially when it comes to the younger generation. For example, in downtown Austin, electric scooters are all the rage. I predict that within fifteen years we will see flying cars. It's exciting and a bit overwhelming at the same time.

2

THE GOOD, THE BAD, AND THE UGLY

"Pour yourself a drink, put on some lipstick, and pull yourself together."
—Liz Taylor

Let's start with the ugly part of the car business to get it out of the way. Unscrupulous salespeople (in any industry but specifically in the automotive industry) have given those of us who genuinely want to serve our customers a bad name. These individuals are going to try to take advantage of you, period. Believe me, I've been in situations where you I didn't know any better, and it's cost me thousands and thousands of dollars. That's why you need to be prepared. You need to be on your A-game when going into the dealership. It's one thing to get a fair deal and another to pay way too much.

FIERCE Girl's Car Buying Hack

Thanks to smartphones, you can check out the reputation of your salesperson the minute you meet them. Go to Facebook and do a quick look-up on him or her. Is he upstanding online, or vile and disgusting?
If they are the latter, you can ask the General manager to pair you up with a different salesperson.

Ladies, I want you to use your superpower, your maternal intuition when it comes to who you're sitting in front of. If they make you feel inferior in any way—don't allow you to ask questions, cut you off every other word, speak over you, or ignore you—STAND UP and walk away. I have seen customers do it in my own dealership. Don't feel like you don't want to hurt anyone's feelings or get them in trouble. Simply request a different salesperson. It's that easy, I promise.

Then get back to what you arrived to do, and buy a beautiful new car. You have the power; own it!

The bad part of the car business is paying the right price but not being able to truly afford it. Know your budget long before you start figuring out your total or monthly payment. It's been my experience that customers often have champagne taste but beer budget. They want a vehicle that is way out of their budget, but because the bank can justify the loan amount, they purchase it anyway, knowing full well that they won't be able to go to that extra movie, purchase that extra wardrobe essential, or enjoy those extra few visits to Starbucks—all because they wanted the more expensive car. They then develop the dreaded buyer's remorse where, within a month, she's looking at her monthly payment and thinking, "What did I get myself into?"

I implore you do not fall into this trap. It's not the dealer's fault, and it's not the bank's fault when it does happen. It's the customer's fault. Take ownership if you're going to bite off more than you can chew. At some point, you have to take responsibility for your choices. It's never fun to tell a customer months into her car payments that, as all cars do, her car has been depreciating and it's no longer worth as much as she owes.

Finally, we come to the good part of the industry. Car buying can be so much fun! If you've done your homework —and it's not really that much homework—you can have an incredible time searching for and purchasing your next dream car. The experience of being able to test drive any make and model in order to figure out what you enjoy driving or can see yourself is for the next few years is really enjoyable. Visualize yourself going off-road, to the mall, to an event, or into your garage. As yourself, "What can I see myself in for the next five to ten years?"

Being able to see your husband, wife, or partner feeling so excited in their new vehicle is an experience, right? They've gotten a brand-new piece of machinery that they can drive around and that can take them places they've never been before, or places they've already been but they want to look and feel good arriving in their new vehicle. There are also those customers who have been in the same vehicle for ten years, and the dreaded car has been breaking down. In this case, getting into a newer and more reliable vehicle is one of the best feelings in the world. I've experienced it personally—having driven a little beater for years—and going in and buying my new vehicle, one that no one else had ever owned, was an incredible experience. I felt good, and I looked good. The confidence that comes from owning a new vehicle is pretty incredible.

One of the best parts of this process is getting to enjoy the vehicle and then seeing your kids' faces or friends' faces when they see the new vehicle that they're going to get to ride in. All the new gadgets and gizmos, the new technology, and the ride and drive of the vehicle are equally exciting. And don't forget that new car smell!

3

WHY WOMEN?

"I like my money right where I can see it: hanging in my closet."
—*Carrie Bradshaw*

My goal is for you to be able to confidently walk into a dealership, know exactly what you want, know how you're going to negotiate, and know how much you will spend on the car of your dreams. I know it sounds a little idealistic, but it's why Cars Her Way exists. It doesn't matter where I travel across the country. When I tell people—both men and women—that I'm the founder and CEO of Cars Her Way, they immediately have a story ready to tell me about a terrible car buying experience they had. So many times, the story concludes with the name of a co-worker, male counterpart, or friend they insist on bringing with them from that point forward.

My own worst car-buying story occurred in 2004. At that time, I was the CEO of our mortgage company. We were a $100-million-a-year company, and I was in charge. President Bush had just announced post-9/11 tax breaks for business owners whose vehicle met certain criteria. As the car gods would have it, the car I had been dreaming of for over a year had just launched, and it met *all* the criteria for me to be able to write off 100 percent of it through our company. I was jazzed (to say the least).

I called my hubby to let him know I was going down to the dealership to stake my claim on one of those beauties. He offered to come for moral support, but I wanted to have the time to walk around, ponder the colors, and bask in the glory of my dream car.

Enter the car salesman.

"Can I help you?" he asked. So typical—he didn't shake my hand or ask my name. He made no attempt to personally connect with me. I proceeded to introduce myself and tell him what I was looking to buy. Are you ready for his response?

"Did you bring your husband with you today?"

"No, I didn't," I replied, knowing exactly where this conversation was going to go, which was nowhere.

Trying not to let my frustration show, I asked if I could test drive the car on the showroom floor. He responded, "We only let *real* buyers drive these high-dollar machines." That was it! This guy was about to get it with both barrels, and he did. I took my check and bought from another dealership in another town, after which point I sent the GM of the other dealership my purchase order as well as a *very* long letter. It's too bad there was no social media back then. My dear reader, I believe that I have lived and experienced every single aggravation you have when it comes to buying a new car, but that story was one for my record books.

I continue to research the automotive industry and speak with subject matter experts about ways to create wins for the industry and female consumers alike. One expert, Katie Mares, shared with me:

> *In all industries, regardless of the service they provide or the product they sell, one thing never changes: organizations are serving and selling to humans, and women are at the helm. Closing the experience gap is critical to captivating and keeping your customer's attention. Everyone has the ability to compare the price and quality of virtually any product or service; once the consumer have done their research, the only thing left to do is create an emotional connection and make that experience the differentiator. This is an important fact to note for all consumers, however it is vital to winning over the vote of the Chief Purchasing Officer (the woman).*

This may sound stereotypical and, in some sense, it may actually be. But I want you to consider this: physiologically, your limbic system as a woman is double the size of your male counterpart. This makes the emotional connection you may be seeking when making a purchase even more prevalent. Therefore, unless some sort of trust is able to be established between an organization and you as the consumer, you are likely not going to be compelled to say yes.

Here's a fun fact: a recent survey conducted by beauty e-tailer SkinStore showed that women in the United States spend about $300,000 *just* on their face during their lifetime. $300,000—let that sink in. We are the most powerful influencer in the world, and it's time to confidently take our seat at the table.

There is a Big Hill to Climb

Ninety-one percent of women report feeling misunderstood by advertisers, and companies—especially those in industries like automotive—are still not ready for the female consumer, even though she has been quietly gaining momentum in terms of the influence she has both in the professional space and in her own backyard, her home.

Marketers and executives *think* they know what women want, need, desire, and dream, but women who work with or for a company that has women positioned at the top levels have a better chance of succeeding. That said, the statistics still haven't changed enough; men still hold eighty-five percent of executive positions. With this statistic in place, organizations don't have a fighting chance of understanding what the female consumer really expects.

Women are different. Period. Right down to our cellular and molecular level. The saying "Men are from Mars, Women are from Venus" couldn't be truer. And, if organizations want to make a true impact in terms of the experience they provide the female consumer, it is critical that they know and understand these differences and are intentional in the design of their female customers' buying experiences. The trek in this upward battle begins with companies being willing to take a step back and truly try to understand the needs, wants, and desires of the female consumer.

What Makes Women Different?

There are behavioral differences between men and women as well as differences in their expectations when interacting with a brand. These differences can be scientifically linked to the physiological differences between men and women.

Both genders have distinct expectations, and it's up to organizations and companies to identify how to best tailor an experience that works for both men *and* women. In my experience, if you build a brand experience keeping women in mind, men will more than likely be satisfied with the experience provided. However, if you build an experience specifically for the male customer, the female customer will not be satisfied in the slightest. I always urge my clients and partners to build their experience with women in mind.

As I noted earlier, research shows the size of the limbic portion of a woman's brain (the part of the brain that controls emotions and memory) to be double the size of the man's limbic brain. As women, we don't tend to make decisions based on logic. Rather, we make decisions based on feelings. We need to feel good when interacting with a brand. The kind of relationship we cultivate with a brand leads to trust and, ultimately, brand loyalty.

Another distinct difference between men and women is the way they communicate. Women crave connection, and one of the fastest ways to cultivate connection is through conversation. Women are master communicators. We use both sides of their brain to communicate, while men use only one. Women can interpret vast amounts of information, all while being present and compassionate in our interactions. While it may or may not be fair, women instinctively know how to communicate, and we expect brands to know how to communicate with us—in the context of a brick and mortar experience.

We enjoy building relationships with the brands we interact with. We need to be able to communicate how we're feeling as well as what we want and expect from a brand.

Brands need to realize the degree of influence women have and work to design an experience that intentionally builds relationships and trust with women. They are, after all, the world's most influential consumer.

If you're on the brand side of this equation, the first step to designing an experience for the female consumer is to realize that her perception is her reality. Companies must focus on what she needs and wants—not merely what they *think* she needs and wants—in order to start to close the experience gap.

I'm frequently asked why I"m so focused on female consumers and why it's so important to me to empower them with the information that they need. Let me be very clear. I don't believe for one minute that we don't know how to negotiate or cut a good deal, or that we are afraid to go to buy a new car without a bodyguard or significant other. I fundamentally believe that women simply don't like the car buying experience. The fact that we often compare car shopping to getting a root canal confirms that theory. I believe with all of my heart that if women truly enjoyed the car-buying experience, we could create *the* economic stimulus package the auto industry desperately needs. We are creatures who love to shop! And any brand looking to grow would do well to recognize that fact.

Keep in mind that, just as male nurses weren't the norm a few decades ago, female car salespeople are often met with a bit of resistance from male customers. As a female car salesperson, I certainly had a tough time working with some of my older male customers. I remember one in particular; let's call him Tony. Tony used to come by my dealership every week when we were located at The Domain. He was quite a colorful character and quite the Italian car enthusiast. Tony owned an extensive car collection, from junkers to pretty cool rides. He was retired and loved to come sit in my office and talk for hours about how he restored old cars. He taught me so much about the Italian culture and the history of Italian cars, and was waiting anxiously for the new Alfa Romeo 4C to launch. He studied the brand and followed the press. In fact, he told me things about the model even before I knew them. He knew that our dealership would receive some of the first cars shipped to the USA. So, after a not-so-patient two-year wait for the return of the beautiful Alfa, I was able to call Tony and let him know it was time to put his name on one of these beauties. He told me he would come by to discuss it.

As planned, Tony showed up at 2:00pm sharp. We went to my office, and when I was pulling out a purchase order to start the paperwork, Tony said, "Now Lisa, if something mechanically goes wrong with this car, what are you going to do?" I was a bit taken aback and said, "Tony, if that happened, I would call my Alfa Romeo tech and ask him for assistance."

Tony replied, "I was worried about that the whole way over here. Women don't know much about cars, and I really want to do business with you, but I need to know that a man is going to service my car." If I hadn't had a two-year-long customer relationship with Tony, knew the names of his grandkids, and accepted both birthday and Christmas gifts from him, I would have punched him in the face.

I reminded him, "I *am* the boss, and if you ever have a problem, the buck stops with me." I assured him that I would ensure he had all the support he would ever need from myself and my service department. I knew Tony never intended to insult me. He had become a friend. But he truly couldn't reconcile doing business with a woman, especially a female car dealer. I have met "Tony" many times during my career in the form of men who didn't believe I'd earned my position and men who didn't support me. And let's be real, double standards are alive and well in the automotive industry. But, through thirty years of trials and tribulations in this industry, my female consumers have stood the test of time.

The time period during which I was relaunching FIAT to the US was when I really started studying consumer behavior. Creating a business plan for the relaunch of a car that exited the market the first time known as Fix It Again Tony was quite a challenge. Who was our customer even going to be? Luckily, we had a few things leaning in our favor at the time.

Gas was five dollars a gallon, so a small, forty-mile-per-gallon car was attractive to the American consumer. We had a hip and cool factor that seemed to be popular with millennials. I personally was determined to show the automotive sector that a small group of women and millennials could "upset" the industry. When the press learned of my dealership's story, the headlines read "When FIAT Met a Fashionista" and "Personal Drive Led to a FIAT Dealership." It seemed as though the industry had bought in as strongly as we did that things needed to change.

The FIAT brand boasted the industry's first female CEO, Laura Soave. She was hip, young, and ultra cool, and she had great ideas for launching the brand. She enlisted me as her partner in crime on a few projects. In early 2011, three other dealers and I were called to Detroit for a FIAT subcommittee meeting held at Chrysler World Headquarters. I wasn't sure why we were being called to the meeting, but I was there with my proverbial bells on. Laura told us all (I was the only female dealer in the room) that she had a product idea/licensing opportunity for the FIAT. We all had to sign NDAs, after which point she proceeded with a slide show.

The lights were turned off and on the screen was displayed the most beautiful car I had ever seen in my life. She said, "Behold, the limited edition Gucci FIAT." I literally screamed out loud, "OH MY GOD!" I mean, I *screamed*. Really loudly. After I realized what I'd done, I apologized to the room for such an outburst. Laura broke out laughing and said, "That's *exactly* the reaction we were looking for!"

Only 500 of those cars were built. My store sold 131 of them and held the record for the most Gucci FIATS sold. That record was recognized by the then-CEO of FIAT Chrysler Automobiles, Sergio Marchionne. I still love to see those sweet little purses on wheels tooling around Austin. Those were the glory days for this fashionista, where Italian designer met automobile! Oh, and did I mention that I bought one of the first ones? My license plate read, "I (heart) Gucci."

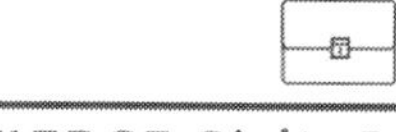

FIERCE Girl's Business Tip

As women, we love beautiful, stylistic, and exotic things. Being in a male dominated- industry initially caused me to believe that I needed to hide my feminine self. I am telling you— you don't. *Be you!* That's what will take your career to the next level and set you aside from your male counterparts (and your female ones as well). Once I learned to truly embrace what I as a female dealer brought to the table, I learned how to meld better with my male counterparts. When I owned my femininity, great projects came my way.

I firmly believe that female car dealers have brought a different perspective to this business. I have a good friend and dealer principal named Liza Borches. Her dealer group, Carter Meyer, has fourteen dealerships in Virginia. All dealers talk frequently about how to elevate their customers' experiences. I fundamentally believe that if all dealership owners were talking to every customer, every time, there would not be a need for this book or this conversation. But they don't. So, what's the solution?

Liza's Philosophy

Our company was founded in 1924, and was led for three generations by three different men by the name of Carter Myers. Then there was me. However, back in the 20s and early 30s, our company was majority owned by my great-aunt, Elizabeth Myers, who worked for Northwestern Mutual Life Insurance.

The story was that in her 20s (in the 1920s), she could call on any executive in New York City and get a meeting regarding their insurance. She alone had enough money to invest in our family company as an outside investor and keep the company alive during the depression. We are not sure that Henry Ford ever knew that one of the Ford dealerships was owned by a woman because that was frowned upon back then. Now, Carter Myers Automotive is female-owned once again and in the fourth generation of our family.

"Having been in business for 95 years, we certainly have had our fair share of ups and downs, but through it all we have had a long history of sharing both profits and ownership with our associates. We believe that our purpose is bigger than just selling and servicing cars.

For our communities, we exist to help families and children get where they want to go in life. Each of our associates has either volunteered time or donated money or gifts to a collective cause this year. When I really look at where we give back, it was all about people. We don't typically support much in the arts or with animals...maybe a bit with Subaru...but in almost every case, we are supporting kids and families in need in our communities. We are looking for ways to help these families move their lives forward, whether by donating a car to a family with a child who is going through cancer treatments or collecting 105 bikes for kids who wouldn't otherwise be getting much for Christmas.

As owners of the company, our associates have complete transparency to our financial results, and understand how taking care of each and every customer comes back to them for a better future. Beth Blalock has been working in our accounting office in Richmond for forty years booking deals, incentives, and handling other office duties. She is the eighth largest stockholder in our company. Karl Soloe is the Parts and Service Director at one of our Honda dealerships and started with us as a technician when he was seventeen. He is the fourth largest stockholder of CMA. Simona Holloway has been selling cars for our company in Charlottesville for thirty-three years and is the twelfth largest stockholder in CMA. Each of these associates have worked hard and contributed to the success of CMA through taking care of customers at a level similar to that of an owner.

Psychology tells us that people take care of the things that they own. Our associates own twenty-six percent of our company, and our General Managers each own up to twenty percent of the dealerships that they run. When everyone has ownership, we are all more incentivized to make sure that we are creating long term win-win relationships with our customers. The goal is to create loyal customers who are our ambassadors in the marketplace and who will never want to go to any other dealership for their transportation needs. As an owner, you would never want to make a short-term decision and take advantage of a customer who would, in turn, never return to your business, never send his friends and family to you, and ultimately hurt your reputation. With all 600 associates having an owner mindset, it allows us to make decisions that will keep us in business for another ninety-five years, not just creating paychecks for today. Everyone wins. Our family, the company, our associates, our customers, and our communities. We may not keep every dollar in our family, but we will make a bigger impact and create more winners in life when everyone has equity in the company. Our mission is to Move Lives Forward for our associates, our customers, and our communities.

FIERCE Girl's Business Tip

Liza is as beautiful as she sounds. She's a mother, a wife, a leader, and a community icon. She truly embodies everything so many of us strive to be. I wanted her to tell her story, but she is very low key and not someone who brags about her accomplishments. She is not that person; I am! I aspire to be more like Liza. But I know that Liza has faced her share of fear and struggles, such as expanding in a down market while being responsible for hundreds of employees and families she cares immensely about. So, as you're out building your own empire, know that fear and doubt are just part of the territory. If Liza can do it, so can you!

Let's talk a bit about your social influence as a woman, which many marketers and business owners—especially those who are men—perhaps haven't fully taken into consideration. Consider the following scenario:

A woman goes into a dealership and has fantastic experience. Her salesperson, who we'll refer to as Sally, has sold her a new car. The customer feels great about the car, and she also feels great about the way Sally treated her and the deal she got. She's now going to jump onto social media to share her experience, because that is what women do. Imagine the impact of the following Facebook post:

"Oh my God, I love my new car! Sally was fantastic! I got a really fair deal and they exceeded my expectations! Hey, Facebook nation, Instagram nation, Twitter nation—if you are looking for a new or used car, go see my friend Sally at ABC Motors. She's amazing!"

That is the power that women have. Not only do we become the customer and friend of salespeople, we also become their brand ambassador, which is so important to the success of a business. That role as brand ambassador is worth millions of dollars to car dealers, and they have yet to figure that out. The other piece they haven't yet fully come to understand is the power of social media when a customer does *not* have a great experience. The same positive enthusiasm that Sally's customer expressed can go in exactly the opposite direction, advising others *not* to visit or purchase from a particular dealership. To be fair, there are a lot of good dealers out there who understand the power of social media, but as women, we hold all the power and all the cards in this area.

FIERCE Girl's Car Buying Hack

Do you want preferential treatment when you're in the service department? Do you want the General Manager to remember your name? Of course you do. So post on social media about how much you *love* the dealership. I had a customer named Twa Rivers, and to say she was a FIAT fan would be a huge understatement. She bought her "Vinnie" and took pictures of that car everywhere she went. She posted and tagged me, the dealership, and FIAT USA. We *all* knew Twa. I am still connected to that amazing lady to this day. Needless to say, when she came in for service, she was a VIP. A little social "sucking up" never hurts!

4

DON'T GO TO THE DEALERSHIP WITHOUT ME

If shopping doesn't make you happy, you're in the wrong shop.
—*Unknown*

My first job in car sales was memorable, and that's putting it mildly. These days, I'm one of the most sought after party guests from within my circle of friends—not necessarily because I myself am terribly entertaining but because I have a million "car business" stories. I almost always open with, "You can't even make this up!"

Remember that when I started out, I was a 19-year-old girl who had never sold anything but skirts. But I knew that the only likely way for me to get a new car after my accident was by getting a demo, working at a car dealership. If I couldn't make that happen, I was going to be taking the bus, and that was most certainly *not* my style as a budding fashionista! The experience was a defining one in my life because I knew it was going to be sink or swim—or, more to the point, walk or take a bus. I had to get the job so that I could get the car. I had to *keep* the job so that I could *keep* the car. I'm still amazed, thinking back to the persistence I had back then. They literally kept passing me around for interviews with department managers because *no one* wanted to hire me. I was only there as a "favor" to Ernie, and they were resentful that they had to try to find a spot for this young fashion major.

After interview number six, I was hired. The sales manager who got stuck with me looked me in the eye and said, "If you want to keep this job, you need to sell at least fourteen cars a month. If you can't, you're going to be out. Do we understand each other?" I made the mistake of asking him when my first day of training would be. After all, I had a two-week training program at Contempo Casuals during which I learned how to properly greet customers, merchandise the racks and windows, clear the dressing rooms, and make suggestions for upselling our clients. I figured that learning how to properly sell a car would surely take a least a month. He looked at me like I was crazy and said, "You will shadow Ernie, and if you ever actually land a customer, we will go from there."

I hate to say this, but at some dealerships, nothing has changed. Have you ever felt like you know more about the car you are considering buying than your salesperson does? That's part of the problem that I believe exists in the automotive industry today, and it's due to a strong lack of training. The turnover rate at most dealerships is as high as eighty percent every twelve months. In order to give dealers the benefit of the doubt, let's assume that eighty percent of salespeople are trained on product knowledge, at least on some level. What's most dealerships *aren't* training their employees on is the experiential side of selling vehicles: properly greeting a customer, asking about their desires and must-haves, *not* putting them through a three-hour back and forth nightmare with the man or woman "in the tower," having efficient time management skills, and *most* importantly, treating female consumers with the respect they deserve. The other major downfall to such a high turnover rate on the showroom floor is that when a customer returns to the dealership six months or a year after her purchase, her salesperson is no longer there. It's frustrating to have to start over when in the middle of a time of need. We call it being orphaned. If you find yourself in this situation ask to see the General Manager and they can reassign you to another (probably) new salesperson. It's better than trying to go it alone.

I observed the way men treated customers when they came in the front door. I also observed the way they treated female customers specifically. I learned early on in my career that you can't judge a book by its cover. I knew that it was my job solely to assist people with their transportation needs. I believed that if I could help them find the perfect car, the rest would take care of itself, and did it ever. I was able to create a huge base of raving fans, customers who trusted me enough to send me their friends and their relatives.

I had one customer early in my automotive career who I will never forget. His name was Kevin, and he owned a large hair salon in Dallas. Imagine Dallas in 1985. This fabulously flamboyant man came into the dealership with the most beautiful hair I'd ever seen in my life—long, frosted, and fabulous. I was standing at the front door when he entered the dealership. My first thought was, "I wonder who does his hair?" I immediately jumped up and greet him and found it strange that no one else did. It was usually a race to the front door to grab customers. I said, "Hi. My name's Lisa.

Welcome to Jim Johnson Chevrolet. How can I help you?" He looked at me, a bit taken back, and he said, "You're a car salesperson?" I replied, "Of course! What kind of car are you looking for?" He said he was looking for a new Corvette, and I took him out to show him our line of Corvettes with only one thought running through my head: when would it be the proper time to ask him who his stylist was?

We had over 200 Corvettes in stock. So, after we walked and talked and looked at the cars, I grabbed the keys to the one he wanted to test drive. While on the drive, he said, "I've been to your dealership seven times, and nobody has ever spoken to me or offered me a test drive. Thank you!" In this moment, I knew I was exactly where I needed to be. Of course, young and naive, I asked why he believed no one had ever been of help to him before. He said, "The cowboys that work at this store don't like gays." I told him I was a fashion major, all my friends were gay, and I thought he was fabulous! It was in that moment I had the courage to ask who did his hair. He told me that he owned a large salon in North Dallas, and even though he hadn't taken on new clients in years, I'd just made his VIP client list.

I brought him inside the building and we sat down and talked about the numbers. I wrote up an official proposal and took it into my sales manager. I was beyond excited. It was the first Corvette I had ever sold *and* I was Kevin's newest VIP client. *Score!*

My sales manager said, "I've seen this guy before."

"Yeah," I replied. "He told me he's been here seven times, and nobody's ever helped him." My manager looked straight at me and said, "That guy's not going to buy a car. He's wasting your time and burning our gas joy-riding around in our Corvette. Get rid of him!"

I was so taken back and visibly upset by the way he was

speaking about my new client, stylist, and, most importantly, friend. After I recovered a bit (girls are *not* allowed to cry in this industry) I said, "Well, actually, I have a cash offer for you, and he wants to take it home today. He has offered full window sticker and wants to know whether we can take a personal check or need a cashiers check."

My sales manager seemed shocked and, I think, embarrassed. He quickly signed off on the deal, and I returned to my office to shake Kevin's hand and escort him to the finance office.

When he finished the paperwork, I took him outside to his new, beautiful, bright red Corvette. We were both a bit emotional. I was so happy to have proven the men I worked with wrong. I was so happy Kevin got the car of his dreams. But let's be real—I was *ecstatic* that Kevin was going to be my hairstylist! Kevin was grateful for the fact that I actually took care of him, that I didn't treat him as though he were different from any other consumer. He also started doing my hair, and I built a great relationship with him and his friends. Over the following two years, I sold them over forty cars collectively. Kevin's referrals were the best customers. They already trusted me as their automotive consultant, not just their car salesman.

Never judge a book by its cover. Kevin had a beautiful cover, and that's why I was attracted to him as both a person and a client. I see so many sales professionals make a decision about whether to serve a client simply by looking at them—looking at the car they drive, the clothes they wear, the hairstyle they sport. Another metaphorical "book" I decided not to judge almost became president of the United States.

A small man drove up in a Chevrolet Caprice Classic. He got out of the car in his navy suit, shined shoes, and military-style haircut. The first thing out of one of the salesmen's mouths was, "That car has vinyl seats, someone else help him." In typical form, I jumped up and greeted him. He was very professional and wanted to get straight to the point: he was there to look at the new Chevrolet Caprice Classics. He introduced himself as Ross Perot, the CEO of Electronic Data Systems (EDS). Honestly, I wasn't sure exactly who he was, but I cheerfully helped him out anyway. He was a man of few words, and he wanted specs along with the name of someone his purchasing manager could call to order over 100 new cars for his employees. Before anyone gets too excited, the deal was moved to our fleet department and I received only a small commission. But in 1992, I did vote for him for president. Why? Because I knew him once upon a time! From the greatest hairstylist to a US presidential hopeful, I learned at an early age treat *everyone* well and value the fact that they decided to walk through our front doors. Every single person you have the opportunity to speak with has value.

When it comes to servicing cars, there are a few entrepreneurial women who decided to cash in as well. Girls Auto Clinic (GAC) is a woman-owned-and-operated business that caters to women. GAC offers automotive repair, resources, products, and services based on trust, education, inclusion, and empowerment. Patrice Banks was a self-proclaimed Auto Airhead® who created educational resources such as car care workshops, car care tips via blogs and vlogs, a #sheCANic (car savvy lady) community, and a Girls Auto Clinic Glove Box Guide to make women more confident drivers as well as smarter consumers.

Patricia created the life and business of her dreams solving a very basic problem: women *hate* going taking their cars to the service department. Not loving what you're doing these days? If not, keep reading because not only am I telling you how to get a smoking deal on a car, I'm teaching you the hacks that have taken me over thirty years to learn. My dream is that, between my radio show on news radio 740 KTRH Houston, my books, and my live appearances, I can encourage both women and men to live the lives of their dreams—and drive a really nice car while doing it.

5

WE LOVE TO SHOP, SO WHY DO WE HATE CAR SHOPPING?

"It took me quite a long time to develop a voice and now that I have it, I am not going to be silent."
—Madeleine Albright

The results of a 2018 online poll conducted by CDK Global that surveyed 64,000 women found that "forty-three percent of women do not trust the auto industry." We've known for years that women buy their own cars and influence around eighty-five percent of all vehicle purchases. So why are they using words like "stressed," "overwhelmed," "taken advantage of," and "panic" when talking about their previous car buying experiences? Perhaps more importantly, how does the industry change that experience for the better? Cars Her Way is, as a brand, committed to changing the female car buying experience by introducing our clients to vetted, trusted automobile retailers.

Car dealerships have long had a reputation for being sexist. A couple of years ago, Anne Mulcahy, the former CEO of Xerox, recounted an experience to *Forbes* magazine during which a Porsche salesman asked her before she made the purchase, "Don't you have to talk to someone about that first?" She responded: "If you don't start working on the paperwork in the next ten seconds, I'll drive thirty minutes to the next Porsche dealer and buy the car there."

Mary Barra, the CEO and chairperson of General Motors, takes those claims very seriously.

"I think it's huge," she told MarieClaire.com. "An environment where customers feel they're going to be respected, they're going to be listened to--that's going to guide how vehicles are presented or how we talk about the vehicles." In fact, there are 2,200 female engineers at GM, and five of the twelve members of the board of directors are women. (Over at their competitor, Ford, two out of fifteen board members are women, and 26 percent of their salaried global workforce is female.)[3]

I had the honor of meeting Mary Barra at the Automotive News Top 100 Women in Automotive Awards in November 2015. She and I were co-recipients. I remember spotting her across the room, and I beelined over to her. When I introduced myself, I was trembling; I knew I was standing in front of greatness. Of course, I wanted to snap a picture with her so I could use it as my social media profile pic, my Christmas card, and everything else I'd need a picture for over the next twelve months. When I asked her if that would be okay, she replied, "Sure! Do you mind if I put on some lipstick first?" She was absolutely kind and warm, and she congratulated me on the award. She knew the story behind my FIAT dealership launch and made it a point to tell me she drove a FIAT around Europe when she was in college. I sat back in my assigned seat and thought about how great it would be to work for a leader like Mary Barra.

FIERCE Girl's Car Buying Hack

Check out dealerships before you ever go in. Some of the CHW dealerships are an experience to be had even if you never buy a car! Many have Starbucks, gift shops, and full blown business centers on site. If you love to shop, make the facilities and the perks just as important as everything else the dealer offers.

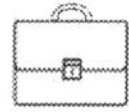

FIERCE Girl's Business Tip

Remember when I asked who you need to meet to change your life or your business? I made sure that evening Mary and I connected personally. There were hundreds of people in the room, but she was the *one person* I knew ahead of time that I wanted to meet. When you have the opportunity to stand in front of greatness, don't waste it. Be intentional in all that you do. It will pay off in spades.

Mary's journey from factory floor to corner office has instilled in her some powerful beliefs.

While a few of those beliefs might sound naïve, they came directly from her experience. She believes that people want to contribute, they want to do a good job, and they're innately driven if given support and tools that encourage them. One piece of advice Mary gives women is, don't give in to fear. Don't let your mind spiral and make assumptions about what the future might hold in terms of your career. Mary's willingness to embrace new ideas might be the reason that GM's setting on a new path. In 2017, the company announced that a focus would be placed on electric vehicles, and it plans to release its first models by 2023. Mary's idea to run a smaller and more profitable automaker is a risk she was brave enough to take, and when you're the first female CEO of one of the country's most influential companies, your risks are bound to pay off.

The way we buy cars is evolving, and for women especially, that's great news. We can do almost all of our research online, where gender is irrelevant. CarsHerWay.com cites a Google report that shows that the amount of time people spend researching a vehicle has gone from 62 days to 71, and a purchase window that was once between 25 and 30 days is now only 10. We're using our keyboards instead of our heels, and dealers are being forced —some kicking and screaming—into a level of transparency, the likes of which has never before been seen. Yet, it's still not enough.

Don't Be Fooled

Sharon Lechter is renowned for her business acumen, and I asked for her financial literacy insights when it comes to car buying because I know they will benefit you.

For starters, she noted, "You may think that the most important issue when buying a car is its price. Think again! Dealers use different tactics to attract you to their lots by advertising 'the lowest' prices. You used to have to spend hours and hours visiting various dealerships, looking at various cars and haggling with multiple salespeople. The internet has changed that forever. You now have the ability to research and comparison shop from the comfort and privacy of your own home, and you can also find qualified dealers who can answer your questions either over the phone or during a test drive." The days of driving to a dealership lot simply because their advertising leads consumers to believe that they have the lowest prices in town are long over!

Consider the Grand Finale

Earlier, I mentioned the finale delivery process I established at my dealership in Austin. Imagine walking into a dealership, purchasing your new vehicle, and being able to bring your friends along for a "fashion show," where your beautiful, brand-new car came down the runway. Imagine your friends standing next to you at the end of this beautiful runway, celebrating with you on the purchase of your new car. There's not a lot that's more fun than getting a brand new car. It's the perfect new accessory to your everyday life! Now you've got it, and your friends are celebrating with you. Isn't that the way it should be? Why every dealer in the country adopted this philosophy is beyond me!

Women like to shop in groups. We like affirmation. We are very, very concerned about other people's opinions. Isn't your best friend, the one who will tell you when a dress makes you look fat? Yes. And she'll also be the one who says, "You look fabulous in that car, darling!"

6

PICK A DEALERSHIP

"Sometimes it's the smallest decisions that can change your life forever."
—Keri Russell

So many people have fallen into the trap of pulling into a big, beautiful, shiny dealership and assuming that they are reputable simply because they have a recognizable brand name or sit on the side of a major highway.

Nothing could be further from the truth. In fact, my Cars Her Way radio show co-host, Chris Martinez, proved this beyond the shadow of a doubt while he was working at Charles Maund Toyota in Austin, Texas. Charles Maund is hardly easily identifiable. It sits underneath a highway underpass, and if you don't know it's there, you're likely to drive right by it. Nevertheless, Chris helped to grow that dealership by approximately 680 percent in seven years, in good part by focusing on properly serving their customers from the time they came in just to look to the day they purchased, each time they came in for service, and beyond.

Customer loyalty is incredibly important to the long-term sustainability and growth of a dealership, and the best dealerships know this and work hard to earn and keep their customers' loyalty. After all, they'd like nothing more than for you to purchase your car from them, take your car to them for service, work with them when you're ready for a new car, and send all of your friends and family to them as well!

Said Elena Ford, Chief Customer Experience Officer for Ford)and the great-great-granddaughter of Henry Ford),

> *One of the biggest drivers of customer experience is: reward my loyalty. The whole point of building a loyalty program is to bring the customers back and keep them in the Ford family.*

When it comes to loyalty programs, manufacturers offer loyalty rebates, so as a customer be sure to ask about this. Some dealers have loyalty points programs. And there are also military rebates and membership programs such as Costco member loyalty and USAA member loyalty. A good dealership will make sure that you are aware of any and all programs that will benefit you.

"Cars Her Way," which is broadcast by iHeartMedia, has sought and continues to seek out the industry's most trusted dealer partners. We are going city by city, and my team is vetting every dealership in town—*every* single one. We have started in Houston, Texas, which is the fourth largest city in the US. Houston has seventeen franchised Toyota dealers, and my team went to work to look for the following:

- Google Rating
- Dealer Rater Reviews

- FaceBook postings and reviews
- Are they members of local chamber of commerce?
- Are they in good standing with the BBB?

Further, we personally inspect the facility to see if (and how) customers are greeted when they enter, the facility as a whole is clean and child-friendly, and the bathrooms are clean (which is a *really* big deal for this gal). What we found was a *huge* disparity in all of these areas.

The way I decide who I will endorse as a trusted partner involves looking at a dealership's website to determine:

- How many years they've been in business
- Whether the store is family owned or owned by a major corporation
- Whether vehicle pricing is listed on the website, for both new and used cars
- Whether pre-owned cars have accurate descriptions
- Whether the sales staff listed, with pictures
- How many female sales professionals work there
- What community awards and accolades the dealership has received
- What professional awards and accolades the dealership has received
- Whether the senior management is listed and whether their direct phone number is provided
- Whether the service department has loaner cars

As we expand our efforts into Austin, Dallas, San Antonio, and then nationwide (in 2020), we are committed to *not* wavering on our overall vetting criteria. I highly suggest that you use the same criteria we use when you're determining which dealership you want to approach first. The information truly is easy to find, so I suppose what I'm advising is, "Do your homework." You will be very happy that you did!

I recognize that, at least as a starting point, many consumers look at online reviews. One thing I would like to say about reviews is that, as a former automotive dealer, I know without doubt that no dealership can make all of the people happy all of the time. I used to tell my team that problems are actually *good* to have. I believe that the moment a problem is encountered is the moment when our customers have an opportunity to see what you're made of —in our case, that we weren't just a car dealership making empty promises. We were an organization that cared, and if our customers had a problem, we had a problem. So, when you are doing your investigation, look at the way a dealership resolves online issues. Do they address them or do they ignore them? That, in and of itself, will tell you a lot about that business.

When we're vetting dealerships for Cars Her Way, we ask for referrals from other dealers in addition to referrals from customers. We have found a few things to be consistent in our quest to find the most trusted dealer partners. Most notably, everyone seems to know who the good guys and gals are, and they also know which dealerships are "Buyer Beware" establishments.

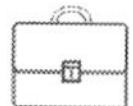

FIERCE Girl's Business Tip

You must take care of business. In business and in life, little things can turn into big things. Make sure that you keep a watchful eye on your online reviews and reputation and, just as your dealer will ask you to do for them, ask *your* clients for reviews and recommendations.

FIERCE Girl's Car Buying Hack

Visit the dealership's bathroom first. If it's dirty, get the hell out of there. The majority of the CHW dealers have full-time staff responsible for cleaning during the dealership's hours of operation. Attention to detail tells a lot about any establishment, and if they are not paying attention to the small things (like a bathroom), it's a good indicator that many other things will likely fall through the cracks, which will ultimately cause you nothing but grief and concern. Another reason we won't partner with a dealership is that they have gravel parking or sales lots. I mean, seriously, do they think I want my heels ruined? You have the choice, so choose a dealership that goes the distance to make sure they wow you at every turn.

One of the best ways to choose a dealership you're likely to have a good experience with is to seek dealership recommendations from your tribe. Post on social media something to the effect of, "Hey gang, thinking about buying a new Ford today. Anybody have any recommendations of a great dealership or a great salesperson?" You're going to hear the good, the bad, and the ugly in the comments. Again, this is the power of social media! There is also a great site called DealerRater that has verified consumer testimonials about both the sales and service departments for dealerships. It's a fantastic resource.

7

PICK A CAR

"If you don't look back at your car after you park it, you own the wrong car."
—Unknown

I believe that the car we drive says everything about us. Ellen Degeneres made a statement once that I constantly repeat: "I won't judge you by the color of your skin, your education, or your politics, but I *will* judge you by the car you drive!" The world would be a kinder place if we all adopted this philosophy, would it not?

According to a 2017 study conducted by Women-Drivers.com[5], the top nine reported emotions experienced when purchasing a car are:

1. Excited
2. Relaxed
3. Confident
4. Apprehensive
5. Nervous
6. Overwhelmed

7. Intimidated
8. Confused
9. Frustrated

Emotions are at the heart of buying a car. While confidence is rising and is now the number three emotion women report (up from number four the previous year), what works best for dealers is actually taking the time to incorporate programs that actively boost confidence in prospective buyers. This means that they take the time and make the effort to ensure that their dealership is a trusted destination, just as we discussed in the previous chapter.

The benefits of this approach don't end the moment a woman finalizes her car sale. She will own that car for another five to eight years, and she will likely choose to service her car at the store she trusts. A confident, happy buyer who has written a great review of her experience with a specific dealer can influence countless other women to follow her lead—for both her purchase and her subsequent service needs. And, when she decides to purchase another new car, the loyalty created will bring her back into the showroom to start the process all over again.

The same study noted that the top 10 reasons behind the decision to purchase a vehicle, in order of importance, are:

1. Price
2. Brand/Model/Reputation
3. Style/Design
4. Safety
5. Space/Functionality
6. Warranty
7. Color
8. Tech Gadgets

9. Mileage
10. Dealership Service

Dealers' relationships with customers, reputation, and standing in the community demonstrate their trustworthiness. Client retention has everything to do with a customer's experience, from the moment she walks through the door, to the purchase of the vehicle, to the way she is treated over the years. Her eagerness to do business again at the same dealership or refer a friend or family member to the dealership in the future hinges on her experience in these areas. In fact, 26.5 percent of women report being referred by a friend or family member when they choose to purchase a car at a specific dealership.

In fact, women pay attention to dealer reviews, on average, fifty percent more than men do. They are looking for authentic reviews written by other women that help them relate to a dealership as a trusted business. Using a strong "evidence-driven reputation strategy" to distinguish your dealership with leads from your BDC (Business Development Center) is highly effective.

Let's have some fun and learn a bit about what your preferred car color says about your style. I have a fashion background, after all!

Black: *Powerful , classy, chic. Black is the most popular choice within the luxury market.*

Yellow: Bold, outrageous, no fear of judgement. You are a trend setter and you're ready to tackle life head-on.

. . .

Brown: You're real and down to earth. You like to be understated but are ready to take on the world.

White: You're elegant, sophisticated, and pure as the driven snow (I drive a white car). White hides imperfections, but that doesn't matter. When you drive a white car, you like everything to be perfect!

Blue: Confident, credible, and authoritative. You believe in order and you are not flashy. You carry a quiet power.

Red: Only word word, ladies: "FIERCE." You are sexy, unabashed, and ready for whatever life brings you.

Silver/Gray: You are modest and don't like to draw attention to yourself. But don't fret, silver is the third most popular color in the US because it's futuristic. So here's to the future!

Baby Blue: You love all things retro and iconic. You're fun and easy going. Nothing rattles you; you go with the flow.

Orange: You are either a Texas Longhorn, a Tennessee Volunteer, or someone who is unique, artsy, and a lifestyle enthusiast.

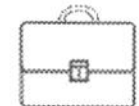

FIERCE Girl's Business Tip

Make sure you choose a car that displays who you are both in business and in your personal life. Do you use your car to take clients out? When you show up for a meeting, do you want to make a statement when you drive up? Be sure to take all of this into consideration before you buy a lime green crossover (not that I have anything against lime green)! Just make sure your new car is consistent with your professional image if you will be using it at all for that purpose.

FIERCE Girl's Car Buying Hack

If you don't see the color you like by the brand you want to buy, don't fret. There are some amazing wraps nowadays that are designed and installed in such a way that you absolutely *cannot* tell the difference between it and paint. The most fun aspect of this technology is that when you get sick of that pink car, you can change it up!

Assess Your Needs

Which car is the "right" car for you at any point in time depends on who you are and what you expect from a car at that point in your life. Some of us like to make a statement with our cars ("I am earth-friendly," "I am a diva," "I am a soccer mom," etc. Some of you just have that need for speed; that's the category I fall into! Give me more horsepower and a loud engine! You need to decide whether your practical side or your wild side will take over when determining what your next ride should be.

For those who need a vehicle that accommodates your regular nine-to-five life, you might want to let functionality trump flash. Here are some practical considerations to keep in mind:

- How many passengers do you need to carry?
- What type of driving do you do? Is it primarily highway, surface streets, off-road?
- Do you have a long commute, and because of that, believe that fuel economy is important?
- What are your must-have features? Some examples: backup camera, leather seats, heated and cooled seats, video and TV for kiddos, Apple CarPlay, etc.
- What safety features are important to you? For example, do you want blind-spot monitoring, lane departure warning, and/or automatic emergency braking?
- What cargo capacity do you need?
- Will you be using children's car seats?
- Will you be doing any towing?
- How much garage or parking space do you have?

Another important feature of a vehicle is the wheel drive. The two main types are front wheel drive and rear wheel drive, although there are additional options such as all wheel drive and 4×4. I want to help you understand the similarities and differences between the two *main* types.

Front Wheel Drive

If a vehicle features front wheel drive (FWD), the transmission transfers power from the engine to the front wheels. A great benefit of FWD is that it's cheaper to design and make than other drives, which means the vehicle may be less expensive for consumers. Most of the time, front-wheel drive cars get better gas mileage because the weight of the drivetrain is less than that of a rear-wheel drive vehicle. FWD vehicles also get better traction because the weight of the engine and transmission are over the front wheels. Generally speaking, good traction in snow and rain makes your drive safer than it would be if you were in a vehicle with rear wheel drive (RWD).

The downside of a FWD vehicle is that the handling of it suffers somewhat. While traction is good, one's ability to handle the vehicle while going around corners and curves isn't as strong as it would be in a RWD car, especially at faster speeds. If you do a lot of driving on winding roads, you'll likely notice a difference between the two different types of drive. The FWD won't be as responsive or as nimble on the road as a RWD will be.

Front-wheel drive vehicles may also feature all-wheel drive. In this case, all four wheels get power when needed, which gives you better traction.

Rear Wheel Drive

The operation behind vehicles with rear wheel drive (RWD) is a bit more complicated. Power is transferred from the transmission to the rear wheels by way of a long driveshaft to a differential. RWD vehicles handle much better than front-wheel drive vehicles, which you will notice during curves, turns, and when navigating through heavy traffic. However, traction won't be as good, especially in wet or snowy road conditions.

RWD vehicles are better for towing because the front wheels have better steering without having a ton of weight on them. Plus, with the power transfer and the tongue weight of the trailer, the rear of the vehicle squats, which gives the rear wheels more traction. If you get stuck, adding weight over the rear wheels may help in getting you *un*stuck.

Rear-wheel drive vehicles sometimes feature 4×4 capabilities. When you put the vehicle into 4×4 mode, it will get power to all four wheels as needed.

8

WHEN IS IT TIME TO TRADE?

"Life is a party. Dress for it."
—Audrey Hepburn

This is an age-old question. People ask, "Lisa, at what point do I need a new car?" I like to respond, "Whenever you want one!"

Every year our circumstances change. I spoke in the last chapter about which factors are top-of-mind when women buy cars. Let's now talk about why women trade in their current cars. In short, not only do our circumstances change, cars change. Let's consider some of the reasons we trade cars:

- New Body Style
- Lower interest rate
- Lifestyle change
- Kids go to college
- Family addition
- Technology
- High mileage

- Unreliability

Sometimes, we need a new car simply because we're looking for a new look! I say that in a bit of a tongue-in-cheek manner, but maybe our life circumstances have changed and we're ready for something new. We used to have to tote around two car seats, and now our little ones can sit in the front or the second row without the bulky car seats. Maybe our kids have gone off to college, and it's time to get that great sports car that you've been thinking about for the last eighteen years.

One of my very favorite customers, Ann, came to my office one day. I could tell she was a bit troubled. I had seen that her car was in service, so I figured she wanted to discuss her repairs. She peeked in and asked if she could steal a couple minutes of my time. I had sold Ann and her family over six cars, so I knew them very well. I could tell she was uncomfortable and she finally spit out the reason why.

"Lisa, what would you think if I traded in my SUV for one of those cute FIAT convertibles?" she asked. That's music to any car dealer's ears, but I asked her why because I had a feeling I was going to hear a good story. She said she had just attended her thirtieth high school reunion, and when she walked into the room, she felt like she was the only one who had aged. She proceeded to tell me about all the medical "miracles" her classmates had undergone, and she was feeling old and doughy. After discussing it with her husband, she felt as though she had two choices: a mini face lift and tons of botox, or a cute, new, Italian sports car. I reassured her of her natural beauty, and sent her home in a red convertible she named Gigi. I always got a kick out of seeing her pull into service department. Who says a new, red, Italian sports car can't make any man or woman feel twenty years younger?

According to Kelly Blue Book, the top ten best new technologies for 2019 are:

Connected Mobile Apps

It's not an overstatement to say that the smartphone has changed everything, including the way we interact with our cars. Most carmakers offer some sort of connected smartphone app, though some are better than others. Look for one that lets you remotely lock and unlock the doors, check the status of levels such as fuel and tire pressure, and even remotely start the car to warm things up on a cold winter morning. Also, make sure to ask whether there is a monthly or yearly subscription fee for the service, as these service fees can vary from carmaker to carmaker.

Teen Driver Technology

Handing over the keys to your teenager can be a nerve-wracking experience, but a bit of clever new technology might ease your mind a little bit. Several cars have some type of built-in teen driver limitations that can notify you if the car is driven over a certain speed, disable the stereo if seatbelts aren't being used, and even keep the stereo from being turned up past level seven.

Chevrolet's Teen Driver feature also offers a report card that will notify parents if safety systems such as the ABS or forward collision alert have been triggered while Junior was behind the wheel.

. . .

Stolen Vehicle Tracking Software

Experts estimate that more than 750,000 motor vehicles will be stolen in 2019. While that number sounds alarming, nearly 46 percent of those vehicles will be recovered—and that number continues to improve. Much of the credit goes to innovative technology that automakers are building into their vehicles, such as the ability for the stolen car or truck to tell law enforcement where it is being held.

The technology is bundled into the vehicle's assistance and security systems, such as BMW's Connected Drive or GM's OnStar. While those advertised features allow effortless diagnostics, concierge, and post-crash notification for summoning rescue services, they may also be used by law enforcement to pinpoint the exact location of a vehicle that is no longer in the owner's possession. Criminals beware!

Apple CarPlay and Android Auto

Though they loathe to admit it, many manufacturer infotainment systems—the do-it-all screens that control stereo, navigation, and climate control—aren't very user-friendly. That's why we like Apple's CarPlay and Google's Android Auto. Plug in your smartphone and it takes over that big screen, replacing it with something that looks a lot more familiar and easy to use.

These apps provide a simplified control scheme from which you can access your music, maps, and phone's built-in voice-control features while avoiding the unnecessarily complicated system that comes with the car. Essentially every manufacturer has promised support for at least one or both Apple and Google's systems, but not all trim levels will support them. Make sure to verify that the car you're preparing to purchase has the right options and that it matches with your mobile devices.

Adaptive Cruise Control

Commuting is no fun. But advanced driver assist systems such as adaptive cruise control can take a lot of the stress out of the experience. By using an array of sensors built into the car, adaptive cruise control can match the speed of the car in front of you so that you won't need to constantly hit the gas or brake in highway traffic.

Some systems even allow the car to be brought to a complete halt and then resume automatically, making stop-and-go traffic considerably less frustrating. It might make you uneasy to hand over some amount of control to the car, but we promise, use it once, and you'll never want to go back.

Exit Warning to Protect Cyclists

People riding bicycles in congested urban areas are often as concerned with parked vehicles as they are with the vehicles on the road. An unexpected opening car door spells doom for cyclists and injury for hapless passengers. Automakers are beginning to address this common danger with rear-looking sensors that detect approaching bicycles and traffic.

The systems are engineered to work for several minutes after the engine has been turned off. If the sensors see an approaching bicyclist or close vehicle, they alert the passenger with a series of bright lights. If the warning is ignored, the most advanced systems will physically lock the door to prevent it from being swung open into the path of the approaching object.

Rear Cross-Traffic Alert

Parking lots are extremely common sites for low-speed —but pricey—car crashes. Backing out of a parking spot, even with a rearview backup camera, can be a perilous exercise. That's why rear-cross traffic alert is so useful.

Thanks to sensors built into the rear of the car, the system can alert you to approaching vehicles, shopping carts, or pedestrians who might have wandered behind your car without you noticing. Loud beeps are standard with these systems, but some cars can even automatically brake before a collision occurs.

Lane Departure Warning

Distracted driving happens. Whether it's due to a quick glance at the stereo to change the channel or a child urgently requesting your attention, we sometimes pay a little less attention to the road than we should.

Lane departure warning systems use cameras to determine whether a car has drifted across a marked lane line, giving a visual or audible notification (or even a vibration through the seat or steering wheel) that you've moved too far outside your lane. The system turns itself off when you use a turn signal, so there's no fear of accidental engagement.

More advanced technology, sometimes called Lane Keeping Assist, can even help nudge you back into the proper lane, which can be a literal lifesaver if you're heading into oncoming traffic.

. . .

Automatic Emergency Braking

Automatic Emergency Braking (or AEB) uses a variety of sensors to determine whether a forward collision crash is imminent and automatically applies the brakes to diminish the severity or avoid a crash entirely.

The auto industry agreed to make AEB standard in cars by 2022, but many vehicles have it available today. While the technology is extremely good, you absolutely shouldn't rely on it to stop you. It's meant as a last resort when the driver isn't paying attention, and it's extremely alarming when the system does engage. While Apple CarPlay and smartphone apps are important, this one could save your life, so it's worth making it a high priority on your shopping list.

360-Degree Camera

Insurance claims from low-speed crashes are some of the most common in the industry. Because they usually occur during parking, a 360-degree camera system can make life a lot easier for folks who might not realize just how big their new SUV is.

Through a combination of cameras on every side of the car as well as some clever computing power, your car's display can show a virtual top-down view of your surroundings. It can show the sides of your garage, whether you're lined up in the parking spot at the grocery store, and even provide invaluable assistance while parallel parking.

FIERCE Girl's Car Buying Hack

360-degree camera systems are getting less and less expensive and are available even on moderately priced cars these days. If you're in the market for a small hatchback, you might not need this system quite as much, but if you're purchasing a large SUV, you will likely find it invaluable.

Maybe you need to downsize. Maybe you're sick of that minivan look and it's time to upgrade to an SUV or crossover. There are so many reasons why people go out and purchase new cars. But the number one reason I find is the rapid pace at which technology is changing. The topic is very interesting to me. You have better technology in a Hyundai than a Maserati, and so many times, people are looking for the newest, latest, and greatest when it comes to technology because we spend so much time in our cars. Remember the way we all needed to have a smartphone? Now, so many of us are looking for the smart car! There are so many reasons to purchase a new car, and the purpose of this book is to help you enjoy that shopping experience.

9

SELLING YOUR CAR YOURSELF

Generally, you have two options when it comes to selling your car yourself. You can sell to a private party, or you can sell to a dealer. Those buying a new or used car from a dealer often trade in their current vehicle as part of the transaction, mainly because it's convenient. This convenience, however, can come at a cost. If you sell to a dealer, you're getting the wholesale value for the vehicle, whereas if you sell to a private party, you're getting close to the retail value. That difference can equate to as little as $100.00 or as much as several thousand dollars.

CONSIDERATIONS WHEN SELLING ON YOUR OWN

Some points to consider before trying to sell your car by yourself:

What is your time worth?

Time is the greatest asset you have, so if you're going to have to invest hours and hours in the selling of your car when you could be investing that time into your business, your family, or yourself, the potential return on the investment of that time may not be worth it. It's simply something to consider.

How much flexibility do you have?

Keep in mind the fact that your car probably won't sell to the first buyer. Are you ready to drop everything you're doing in order to drive to the 7-11 or nearest gas station so someone can come look at it? You *never* want a stranger coming to your home; always meet a potential buyer in a neutral public location.

You will also need to go to the DMV with the new buyer to make sure they pay the sales tax and registration, and transfer the title into their name, which takes a good amount of time depending on how backed up the DMV is on any particular day, not to mention the time it takes to coordinate your schedule with that of the buyer.

You aren't a bank

Because you aren't a dealership, you don't offer financing. That fact knocks out a lot of potential buyers.

A clean break is a good break (in this case, anyway)

What if something happens to the car? You don't want the purchaser coming back and blaming you for a mechanical failure you knew nothing about.

Do you love marketing?

When you sell a car yourself, you are responsible for advertising it and making sure you know all the disclosure laws for your state.

Remember when I discussed the importance of prepping your car? Whether you're selling to a dealer or to a private party, the better condition your car is in, the better chance you have of getting a fair value from the buyer. When you go to the dealership prepared, you will get what is fair to both you and the dealer/buyer. In full transparency, I have *never* sold a car to a consumer myself. I prefer to trade them in. Between the tax credits and the fact that my time is way too valuable to spend it advertising, showing and negotiating with a private party, I just don't want to mess with it. In most states, you will save on sales tax by selling your car to a dealer. If you trade it to the dealer, you only pay the difference in sales tax between the price of the new car and the value of your trade-in, saving you 8.25 to 10 percent on the trade difference. You'll have to do the math on that, but it seems like a no-brainer to me. If you play it smart, you can shop your trade to potential dealers and receive "buy bids" that are usually good for seven days. There are even websites that will buy your car. All you do is plug in your VIN number, plate number, and mileage and they will pick up the car and bring you a check!

FIERCE Girl's Car Buying Hack

If you are certain that you want options when it comes to

selling your car, there are businesses that will consign your used car and handle the paperwork for you. I haven't seen great success with them, but I want to make sure that you know the option is available. Check with your insurance company if you do decide to go that route. Usually, when you insure a car it has to be garaged at your home, and having it on a car lot could negate your insurance, which would not be good if something happened to the car while it was still on the consignment company's lot. FIERCE girls always do their homework. Better safe than sorry!

Sidenote: As of April 2019, the only states that don't allow sales tax credits are California, DC, Hawaii, Kentucky, Michigan, Montana and Virginia. If you live in the states, you have more incentive to sell your car to a private party.

10

NEW OR USED?

"Coffee in one hand, confidence in the other."
—Unknown

I have so much information and so many feelings about the topic of new versus used vehicles. You should be familiar with the pros and cons of purchasing a used car compared to a new vehicle. Yes, you can save a lot of money, and purchasing a used car is a smart decision given how quickly new cars depreciate. When buying used, you're letting the original owner absorb most of the depreciation costs. However, as cars get older and less valuable, they are also less expensive to insure. Some cars tend to depreciate a lot more quickly than others, so it's smart to pay attention to the residual values when buying a car, whether new *or* used. If a specific car depreciates quickly, you should really lean toward buying a used model. You can check out residual values through Kelly Blue Book.

I sold used cars at my dealership, and my cars had the highest integrity when it came to inspections. Buying a three- to five-year-old car will net you maximum savings, and that's the ideal age at which to purchase a pre-owned vehicle. It's old enough for major depreciation to have taken place, but it's not so old that major performance issues are likely to occur. Plus, there's always a chance that the vehicle could still be covered by warranty.

All that said, there's simply no way to guarantee a problem-free transaction. Since most used cars don't come with a warranty, you could get stuck with expensive repairs. If a used car doesn't come with a warranty, it's not a bad idea to consider purchasing an extended warranty for it. No matter what, it's very important to get a used car thoroughly inspected by a mechanic before purchasing it. Another disadvantage of buying a used car is that you don't have much choice when it comes to colors, styles, and add-ons. You're limited to whatever's on the market, and you may have to shop around for a while in order to find something you like.

If you are going to buy a pre-owned vehicle, I highly recommend buying from a franchised car dealer versus buying off the street or through Craigslist. A dealer is most likely to stand behind the vehicle should you have problems with it, whereas an individual buyer will be gone with the wind. A final disadvantage to a pre-owned vehicle is that you'll have to pay a higher interest rate when financing. Most lenders simply charge a higher rate on used vehicles.

Before you purchase a pre-owned vehicle, have it inspected by a professional mechanic. There are absolutely no exceptions to this recommendation, including certified used cars being sold by a dealer. Don't trust what anyone tells you. Getting the car inspected is not completely foolproof, but it's your best tool when it comes to preventing headaches down the road. Make sure to use a mechanic who specializes in that particular brand. Mobile inspections within which they don't put the car up on a lift are not going to cut it. Also, before paying for the inspection, make sure the car comes back with a clean history report. Most dealers will provide you with a free Carfax or AutoCheck report. If not, it only costs $30 to get one. Keep in mind that they are not always accurate; if an accident was never reported, it will not show up on the report. But I've used reports from these resources myself over the years as a dealer purchasing cars, and I highly recommend them.

Another good option when purchasing a pre-owned car from a franchise car dealer is to look for what we call a CPO. This stands for Certified Pre-Owned. These vehicles have the manufacturer's seal of approval and have gone through a strict inspection program. A typical Certified Pre-Owned car goes through a comprehensive inspection and will have worn parts replaced to meet factory standards. Furthermore, there are age and mileage restrictions that prevent certain vehicles from being eligible for the program at all. Most cars older than five years or with more than 75,000 miles are not eligible. So many of these cars are lease returns purchased at auction or executive cars from the manufacturer.

Most manufacturers offer a twelve- to twenty-four-month extended the warranty on their CPO vehicles, and have some special finance programs in place as well. Only franchised new car dealers are able to sell Certified Pre-Owned vehicles backed by the manufacturer. If you see a "certified car" at a franchised or independently owned used car lot, please know that this is not the same as a Certified Pre-Owned car. Their certification has nothing to do with the manufacturer. It usually indicates simply that they did their own inspection and slapped a "certified" sticker on the windshield to confuse shoppers.

These other "certified" programs are not as attractive or reputable as the manufacturer-backed programs and could leave you at risk if the dealership goes out of business. I'm frequently asked whether Certified Pre-Owned cars are worth the extra cost, and they absolutely are. The advantage to buying a Certified Pre-Owned car is, most notably, the peace of mind you get from the factory-backed warranty and through-and-through inspection. However, it does come at an additional cost of, on average, between $500 and $2000 per car. When it comes to luxury cars, the premiums are even higher. On average, you'll pay $2,000 to $3,000 more for a Certified Pre-Owned luxury vehicle; it depends predominantly on the length and coverage of the warranty.

You could have a used car thoroughly inspected by an independent mechanic and combine that with a factory-backed extended warranty in order to have a nearly Certified Pre-Owned car (just not officially). You need to simply compare the cost of each, and see which one offers you the best deal. In many cases, buying a Certified Pre-Owned car is a great decision, especially if you value the peace of mind that comes along with it. But remember, even if you decide to buy a Certified Pre-Owned car, I advise having an independent mechanic inspect it before you purchase it.

FIERCE Girl's Car Buying Hack

When it comes to purchasing a used vehicle, be sure to ask about a powertrain warranty as many dealers offer a FREE lifetime powertrain warranty. Most of these warranties offer decent coverage if you have major engine failure. Also, in order to qualify for this lifetime powertrain warranty, the car or truck must go through an extensive check, so on many levels, it helps provide you with peace of mind.

Lemon Laws

Consumers often wonder about the degree to which they are protected by Lemon Laws, laws that provide assistance if you purchase a vehicle that repeatedly fails to meet the standards of quality and performance.

Notes Lechter, "Lemon laws may cover more than warranties in your purchase contract, and they vary from state to state. It is best to research the specifics for your state to determine what you are entitled to. For more information visit, http://www.bbb.org/us/auto-line/state-lemon-law.

"The federal government also has a Lemon Law (the Magnuson–Moss Warranty Act), which protects citizens of all states and it covers anything mechanical. If the vehicle is under warranty and you've had problems with it, subjected it to repair, and it has not been resolved, you may find relief from the Magnuson-Moss Act. It applies to vehicles under their original or extended manufacturer's warranty, and your car must be in the shop for three or more times for the same problem. It may include issues with brakes, transmission, suspension, head lights, water leak, paint defect, and more. If you have these issues, you may be able to force the manufacturer to comply with the warranty under this Act. If they refuse, you may want to call a lawyer."

11

BEFORE YOU STEP FOOT IN A DEALERSHIP...

"She remembered who she was and the game changed."
—Lalah Deliah

When you arrive at a dealership to look at cars, do you feel like you have a target on your back? Do you want to become the hunter, not the hunted? Women from all over the country tell me there's nothing worse than pulling up to a car dealership and feeling this way, seeing between four and eight salespeople people standing out front, waiting for them to park. I drove into a dealership lot a couple of weeks ago, and I was literally on the phone when the salesperson came up and knocked on my window.

I rolled down my window and asked, "Can I help you?"

He replied, "Yeah, what are you looking for today?" I just rolled my window back up on him.

There is no worse feeling than the notion that you're simply a number representing a sale. That's something that *has* to change in our industry. So, how do you become the hunter versus the hunted? You start by pulling up to that dealership with a preset appointment. When that guy or gal comes up and knocks on your window while you're finishing a business call, you can say, "No, I don't need anything. I'm here to see Mike." That's step one: arrive at the dealership with a preset appointment.

Second, know what you can truly afford before you visit the dealership. Be sure to use companies like TrueCar.com , AutoTrader.com, Cars.com, or CarsHerWay.com to identify a fair price. There's nothing worse than a consumer trying to negotiate an unrealistic number and then going home empty-handed. The general rule of thumb is that for every $10,000 spent, the customer will incur a $200 a month payment on a sixty-month loan with an interest rate of 7.5 percent. This calculation will help you to quickly determine your approximate payment on a car, and it will prevent you from looking at an Escalade with a Corolla budget. It's not worth the headache to go into a dealership and try to get to that fictional price. Believe me, neither you or the dealer will like it. There simply isn't that amount of margin for the dealership to work with. In fact, for point of transparency, the average new car dealership makes approximately $2,014 per vehicle. $2,000 might seem like a lot to you; I believe it's a fair profit. The automotive retailer likely employs between 50 and 300 people, gives to local charities, and is usually the largest sales tax contributor in your town or county. They help local charities and help to ensure that kids have good schools to attend.

Next, be aware of the concept of negative equity. Notes Kerri Wise, VP of Industry Education and Relations for TrueCar, "Consumers who are in the market for a vehicle in many cases have to first dispose of their current vehicle. While some consumers decide to sell their vehicle [via] private party, many choose to trade it in to a dealer so they avoid the hassle of selling it themselves. Consumers have significant apprehension [toward] the trade appraisal process and the fairness of the value offered by dealerships. This is in part because consumers naturally want the highest value for their trade, and they lack visibility in terms of how dealers determine the trade value offered.

"Consumers are looking for a high level of transparency and visibility in the trade appraisal process. In fact, recent TrueCar research shows that when a dealer conducts a side-by-side trade appraisal with the consumer, the dealer is three times more likely to get a 5-Star rating from the consumer, and the consumer is 1.5 times more likely to sell/trade their vehicle to that dealership.

"Using a trusted 3rd party Trade tool like TrueCar Trade can aid consumers in feeling confident in the value of their trade. With TrueCar Trade, consumers can receive an upfront cash offer for their vehicle online. This is a specific value, not just a range. TrueCar Trade's dynamic interface behaves similarly to TurboTax, with the trade value changing in real-time as the consumer completes a survey about the features and condition of their vehicle. This promotes confidence and educates the consumer on the value-impacting items that add and deduct from the value of their vehicle.

"The consumer is then connected with a TrueCar dealer who will schedule an appointment for a condition confirmation walk-around at the dealership. To connect the dots, the dealer will confirm the vehicle details the consumer entered online using the TrueCar Trade tool. If there is a discrepancy in the vehicle's condition, the dealer can report that in the tool, which will adjust the original value in real time. In the end, the consumer will receive a print out of their universal condition report, which includes their cash offer and a detailed itemization of the specific features and conditions that impacted the value. This level of transparency and validation reduces the typical friction in the process and is a win-win for both the consumer and dealer. Other sites for trade evaluations are:

www.kbb.com
www.autotrader.com
www.CarsHerWay.com

"Negative equity is never fun. It usually happens when you decide to trade in a vehicle too early or buy add-ons like lift kits or the big stereo system. Remember that without a big amount down or excellent credit, it's not going to be easy to get out of that car right away. You're better off waiting, in my opinion, until you can get closer to a breakeven scenario. The worst thing you want to do is continue to keep burying yourself into a vehicle."

I want you to keep in mind that car appraisals are a bit subjective. Depending on what you're trading, here is what a dealer or third party will base their bid on:

1. Scarcity in the market: How many of that vehicle are available within a certain mile radius? (Due to fluctuations in the market, whatever bid you get on these websites is merely a jumping-off point)
2. What is the condition of the interior of the car?
3. Are you a smoker?
4. Does the car have dents and dings?
5. Are your tires on their very last tread?
6. What type of reconditioning is required to resell the car?
7. Is the mileage in line with the model year?
8. Does the car have an old body style?

9. Has the car been discontinued? (Saab, Pontiac, Mercury, Suzuki, Alfa Romeo 4C, etc.)

You want to bring the car to the dealership in the best condition possible because you're asking somebody to buy that car and pay you the maximum amount of money for it. Just as you would not pay top dollar for a dirty car that's been smoked in and is a mess, neither will the dealership. So get that car pristine before you ever bring it to the dealership.

FIERCE Girl's Car Buying Hack

Another great hack I have found for busy women is to take virtual test drives of the cars you're interested in on YouTube. In fact, YouTube is an incredibly valuable resource when it comes to finding cars that you like and it's a mecca of virtual test drives and walkarounds. That will save you a lot of time and aggravation once you get to the dealership.

12

PREPARING TO VISIT THE DEALERSHIP

"The woman who does not require validation from anyone is the most feared individual on the planet."
—Mohadesa Najumi

"What should I bring with me when I go car shopping?" This is an often-asked question. If you're only shopping, bring yourself and a big bottle of water and your walking shoes. This is supposed to be fun. In fact, if you are feeling really adventurous, do it on Saturday morning and call it cardio! My goal is for you to feel armed with knowledge, powerful, and ready to get your shop on!

I hate to admit this, but the fact is that salespeople begin judging you the minute you enter the lot, and their judgement extends to what you're wearing. They're also judging you by the car you're driving when you bring it to trade in, so please take five minutes and run it through the car wash before you arrive at the dealership. Clean out all the junk and trash, and vacuum it. Make it look like a valuable asset, one that the dealer will want to buy from you and pay full value for. This is Merchandising 101! Step out of that car with both you and your car looking like a million bucks. That's how you'll set the proper tone for the rest of the visit.

More important than what you're wearing or driving when you pull into a dealership, I want you to have a viable Plan B that you are prepared to implement. If you are not treated with the respect that you deserve as the number one influencer in the world, that Plan B is to shut your purse, turn around, and walk out of the dealership. There are a lot of options when it comes to automotive retailers in the country as well as all over your city or town, no matter where you live.

In preparation for your dealership visit(s)

Call your bank or credit union for a 10-day payoff amount. Go ahead and do that legwork for the dealership even though the dealership's going to have to do it regardless. If you trade on a Saturday, many times the dealership cannot get through to the bank or credit union to get that accurate payoff. They need to know that 10-day payoff amount so that they can accurately figure out your payments.

You also want you to know your credit score before you walk into the dealership. All financing nowadays, whether it's for a car or a house or even a credit card, is risk-based. That means that it's based on your credit score, so you are a better consumer if you monitor your credit score. Aim to go into the dealership knowing what your middle credit score is (any financing they might provide for you is going to be based on that credit score). Here are a few sites where you can check your score:

www.experian.com

www.freecreditreport.com

Advises Sharon Lechter, pull your own credit report and review it for errors. Know what your credit score is when you visit the dealerships so they can give you more accurate quotes. When the dealerships pull your credit report, it is considered a "hard inquiry," and when combined with other hard inquiries, it may hurt your credit score. However, when multiple inquiries for an auto loan are made in a short time, FICO will treat them all as one inquiry.

Next, I want you to sit down and work your monthly budget. The last thing that you need to do is get in over your head because you're so excited about a car that somebody talks you into buying something, but you can't afford (we've all done it). I want you to know what your monthly budget is and what you are willing to spend on a new car. That's where the research comes in. There's no excuse nowadays for us not to make good consumer decisions and be well informed when buying a car because everything we need is at our fingertips. For reference, I love the website www.everydollar.com for helping with budgeting.

Call your insurance agent. There are so many variables in the insurance business, including whether or not you have teenage drivers or a poor driving record as well as classification of the car you're looking at. For example, if you're going from a minivan to a sports car, there are many reasons why your insurance cost is going to increase. Not only is the car's classification important, so is the fact that the car you're looking at is more valuable. You can check the following sites for insurance guesstimates:

www.esurance.com

ratekick.com

Have in mind your down payment amount before you go to the dealership. So many dealers want to work with you based your monthly payment and down payment, not the final price of the car. Absolutely do not fall into that trap; work your car deal first.

Check out the ratings of both the sales and service departments of the dealership you intend to visit. This is where Google becomes your friend. If the dealership has poor ratings in their sales or their service department, it's time to look for a different dealership.

Go to the dealer's website and see how many women they have selling cars. I'm a firm believer that if women are not working on a dealership's showroom floor and selling cars, there is a problem with either the leadership or the culture! I always encourage my tribe to support dealerships that hire women. I'm not saying that you have to buy cars from only women, but it's sure nice to have options, isn't it?

Call your bank or your credit union about financing options. Many times, dealerships have low APR financing, which we will talk about in a bit. First, let's discuss subvented financing, which is the low-interest rate from the vehicle manufacturer versus a cash rebate. These days, interest rates are quite low. If you have good credit, I always recommend that my clients take the cash rebate versus the subvented financing, even if it is zero percent, the reason being that if something happens to your car, whether it gets wrecked or stolen or you simply want to trade it in, you're always better off having taken the principal reduction upfront, meaning that you'll owe less on that car if something happens. In today's market, with interest rates from banks and credit unions as low as 1.9 percent anyway, this choice often makes the most sense. An informed consumer is a successful consumer.

Nearly every book written on the art of negotiating advises, "Don't play your cards *and* hold back information."

And yet we wonder why it feels so adversarial when we go into the dealership. I equate it to walking into Nordstrom and looking for that great pair of black boots. When the sales associate asks the obvious questions: "What size do you wear? Do you have a budget in mind? Do you want three- or four-inch heels? What's the occasion? What color are you looking for?" it's not the time to hold back on your salesperson! So why in the world would you do that at a car dealership when you're looking to purchase a product that's significantly more expensive than a pair of shoes?

If you want to buy a new house, and your realtor asks, "Do you have a house you'd love to buy?" he or she has the experience while you have the expectation. Both the experience and the expectation must be set upfront. What's your monthly budget? What neighborhood do you want to live in? What school district? Do you tell the realtor you're not going to give them the information they need to find the perfect house for your family? Of course not! So why do the so-called "experts" give consumers wrong advice in this area? When I was thinking about titles for this book, *Myth Busters: The Number One Reason Women Don't Buy Cars* repeatedly came to mind.

SHARON LECHTER'S FINANCING EXERCISE

For a quick understanding of how financing works, select two models of car that you are interested in, one you believe to be moderately priced and the other you consider quite expensive. Use the internet to find two dealers for each vehicle and gather the following information. Understand that actual finance rates will be dependent upon your specific financial issues, but they will probably be advertising base rates that you can list. You may also need to call the dealerships to ask about any special incentives they are offering.

You can recreate the following diagram on a sheet of paper to help you compare dealership options on two different vehicles. You will then be able to assess which dealer is offering the best deal and why.

	Car #1		Car #2	
Make & Model	________		________	
Features	________		________	
	Dealer 1	Dealer 2	Dealer 1	Dealer 2
Price	____	____	____	____
Finance Rate/APR	____	____	____	____
Term of Loan	____	____	____	____
Special Incentives	____	____	____	____
Which dealer offered best deal?	____	____	____	____

I have listed below the items you should bring with you when you go to the dealership. My goal is to empower you to take full control of the deal and your experience.

- Pre-approval letter from your credit union or bank. You can usually do it online, and having a pre-approval letter doesn't obligate you to use that bank or credit union for financing. It just means you've got options.

- A printed trade evaluation from Kelley Blue Book, AutoTrader and/or TrueCar.
- Your checkbook. It gives you just one more reason not to have to come back. Dealerships do not take Venmo.
- Your car insurance card (this is very important). It's has the VIN number of your current car as well as all kinds of other information that the dealership is going to need.
- If you've got a vehicle that is paid for, bring the title in the event that you trade it in.
- All the service records for your trade-in. If you've taken pristine care of your car and had its oil changed every 3,000 to 5,000 miles, you want to show that. Bring all the receipts (you need to be saving them anyway). Again, you're asking this dealership to buy your car for the most money possible. Make it easy on them.
- Your payoff information, including your account number.
- A notebook. Write down the questions that you want to ask so that you don't forget any of them, and then write down their answers.

It's very important to bring the second set of keys for your trade-in. Most people don't know this, but because of all the electronics contained within them, keys cost between $300 and $800 each. If you do not have the second set of keys to your trade-in, the dealer will deduct that, typically from the value of your trade-in. Again, the goal is for you to avoid having to make a second trip.

Finally, bring all copies of your extended warranties and insurance policies that you purchased for your trade-in. Most people don't realize that you can cancel them and get a refund on any unearned premiums.

Sharon Lechter recommends that consumers are extremely clear on their budget as well before they visit the dealership.

She advises, "Many financial experts state that you should spend no more than 20 percent of your net income on a monthly car payment. To determine what that number is, you'll need to figure your total net income (take-home pay after taxes) and then subtract all your fixed expenses. The remaining amount is your net spendable income. By figuring that out, you can then determine what 20 percent is in dollars and cents. You will also remember that your new vehicle may increase your car insurance and fuel costs as well. Gather your financial information needed by the lender for your loan application process. In addition to the above list, take with you:

- Social Security card and driver's license
- Contact information for your employers for the past two years
- All other sources of income
- Your most recent bank statements, for both checking and savings accounts
- Your most recent statements for stocks and brokerage balances
- Current statements for all your debts and contact information for the related creditors
- Explanations for any blemishes on your credit report"

FIERCE Girl's Car Buying Hack

Walk in like you own the place! Hold your head high, look great, and exude excitement about your latest purchase!

FIERCE Girl's Business Tip

As the aforementioned information will prepare you for your car buying process, I also encourage you to take this discipline into your business life. The information in this book can serve as preparation for *all* things that you need to be successful in business. Whether walking into a dealership or a boardroom, be a FIERCE woman, a business woman who is prepared, ready to negotiate your success and hold your ground when you believe that what you're doing matters. Incorporate the tips and lessons from car buying into your business life as well. My goal is to empower you and teach you and for you to know that I'm always rooting for you!

13

GO TO THE CARS, OR HAVE THE CARS BROUGHT TO YOU?

"I don't like to gamble, but if there's one thing I'm willing to bet on, it's myself."
—Beyonce

These days, many automotive retailers are advertising pick-up and delivery services in conjunction with consumers' car buying and servicing experience. I have a definite opinion about this. I love the idea...*when it comes to servicing your vehicle.* My good friend Brian Benstock, who is the Vice President/General Manager at Paragon Honda in Queens, New York, wrote the book on elevating the customer experience by removing the friction involved with dealing with servicing your car.

Brian and I met in 2012 at an industry event in Miami. Brian is a world-class athlete and lives every day to win, in both life and business. He has both mentored and taught me over the years, and we both had an unbridled passion to be number one within our perspective brands.

We took different paths; I was all about the people and culture, and Brian was (and is) an industry leader who adopted technology long before it was cool. He has always stayed ahead of the curve, forming strategic alliances with Google and becoming the thought leader within our industry when it comes to all things disruptive. The smartest thing I did was to align myself with him and his philosophy: "The Future Is Frictionless." I am grateful for his friendship and the way he shares his expertise freely with me and within our industry.

Voice technology allows for a seamless transactional experience for customers. Retailers, both large and small can optimize this channel to assist their customers in a frictionless future.

—Brian Benstock, VP Paragon Honda

FIERCE Girl's Business Tip

Do you want to become a thought leader in your industry? Are you interested in a promotion? I make it a point to attend industry conferences and introduce myself to influencers. I also make myself available to the up-and-comers. I engage in both of these activities because there could be a day when the tides turn, and I need them (or vice versa). I believe that in order to build a strong industry in *any* industry, the leaders must lead (and by leaders, I'm referring to the top performers and top performing companies). It's about survival. Our industry and the businesses within it must stay strong in order to keep our individual businesses strong.

Over the years, I have also found that being seen as a thought leader and all-around good human are great assets when it comes to recruiting strong talent. Align yourself with industry leaders. Watch what they do and how they do it. Be mindful of their strategy. You NEVER want to be the smartest person in the room. I never saw my competitors as evil; in fact, I was best friends with many of them. And why not? None of us will ever succeed without a little help from our friends (and our competition).

When it comes to *shopping* for a new car, I don't understand why anyone would want to limit herself to looking at only one car at a time.

Companies such as Carvana and Carmax are selling convenience, and the entire premise is based upon the foundational approach that they bring the car to a prospective buyer's house. They are reminding you that "car buying doesn't have to suck" and playing on the fact that the number one influencer in the world hates shopping for cars. I will say that, from a marketing standpoint, the approach is brilliant. They are removing the friction between the consumer and the retailer. For you as a consumer, however, they are also removing the joy of the test drive as well as the opportunity to sit in a beautiful new car and walk the lot (we need to get our steps in somehow right?).

The deal is, they drop off the car, let you test drive it for seven days, and then pick it up. While it may initially sound appealing, do not fall into this trap; it absolutely limits your selection. Most of us are not too busy to go to Target or the mall. To further cement my point, imagine that you're heading out to purchase a pair of black boots. When you go into Nordstrom, you see an amazing pair that is different from what you initially had in mind—in fact, you didn't even know this particular design existed. You end up walking out with them, completely thrilled. Purchasing a car is no different of an experience. I don't believe that we should have one car delivered to us, only to sit in the driveway. Once we get used to it, it's easier to settle than to send it back. When we keep it, it's *not* in the name of convenience; it's the result of a marketing ploy. Find the right dealer (a Cars Her Way certified retailer is a great place to start) to do business with. Take your time. This is your second biggest purchase after your house. Walk the lot. Sit in the cars. Take multiple test drives. Savor the experience! If you follow my tips and are efficient with your time, you should be able to get into and out of the dealership within two to three hours.

FIERCE Girl's Car Buying Hack

Many dealerships offer at-home test drives and will send a salesperson to your home in the car you wish to test drive in order to accomplish this. Take advantage of the opportunity if you so choose. BUT, do business with a retailer that wants to elevate the customer experience and is not afraid for you to meet the staff and visit their showroom floor. I think there's a time and place for at-home test drives, but beware that by engaging in one, you are limiting yourself and forgoing what would hopefully be the fun and memorable experience of buying your new car. Choose the right retailer, and you will *want* to go car shopping, I promise. Check out www.carsherway.com for a trusted dealer partner in your area.

Also, remember that you don't have to buy a car on your first visit. Go back a second time and bring a friend or your kids. I don't usually suggest doing that the first time because you want to figure out what *you* want. Many times, bringing everyone with you on the initial shopping trip ends up being more of a distraction than a help. The second time around, bring back the people who are going to be riding in the car with you. See how the car makes them feel.

As inefficient as I believe it is to have multiple cars delivered to the customer and then taken back to the dealership, I do think there's a time and a place to have a car brought to your house, where it can spend the night so you can determine whether or not it's indeed the car of your dreams. Once you've negotiated a deal that you feel great with, tell the salesperson that you want to take the car home overnight. Let them know that you want to park it in your garage and your driveway in order to ensure it properly fits, and you want to drive it around your neighbourhood. Commit to coming back to sign the papers the following day. There's absolutely no need to have multiple cars brought back and forth to your home. In doing so, you're limiting your options. Please trust me on that.

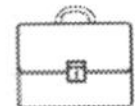

FIERCE Girl's Business Tip

People are willing to sacrifice selection and give up the right to negotiate just so they don't have to go into a car dealership and endure what some people feel is a very uncomfortable process. The smart dealers have figured out that the best way to beat the competition is to offer an elevated consumer experience.

Ladies, I am here to tell you that you *can* have your cake and eat it too. I know car dealers around the country who will cater to you, deliver your car, treat you with the respect you deserve, and allow you to negotiate a price you feel good about. This conviction is the very reason why Cars Her Way and this book exists. I am not very popular with the "bad dealers" right now; I am exposing them. The good dealers are cheering from the rooftops, as they don't want to be lumped in with the bad guys and gals. Be sure to visit Cars Her Way, as we are adding trusted dealer partners daily.

14

START WITH A TEST DRIVE

"If men liked shopping, they'd call it research."
—Cynthia Nelms

Even as children, human beings have a fascination with cars. Have you ever played with Hot Wheels? I love buying them for my grandson, Eli. He has hundreds of them, and we sit on the floor together while he drives them around and tells me all about them. He tells me how fast they are, how expensive they are, and who would most likely drive each of them. As young girls, many of us played with Barbies instead of Matchbox Cars, so we are not as knowledgeable about cars from a young age as our brothers are.

In 2016, I received a call from Proper Television in Canada. They invited me to shoot a pilot of a car show they were considering producing. The show was called "Car Sharks." The premise was that five car dealers (think Shark Tank) would bid against each other to buy the customer's car. Each customer would present and try to sell us his or her car. It was a lot of fun to shoot, and in the process I met and teamed up with one of the coolest automotive experts I have ever met, Bisi Ezerioha, the CEO and Chief Engineer at Bisimoto.

Bisi is an American-born Nigerian engineer. His automotive creations have appeared in numerous films, TV shows, toys (Mattel Matchbox Cars), and video games. He is, quite honestly, one of the most accomplished people I have ever met. We struck up a friendship that we have continued to this day. Recently, he was commissioned by Mattel to build the 50th Anniversary Edition Hot Wheel. As in, the full-size car. Being around Bisi is nothing less than incredibly exciting, and his passion for cars is contagious.

One day on the set, I had a discussion with him about his career versus mine. He told me that he had always wanted to own a car dealership, that he assumed that everyone who came to buy a car must really enjoy the experience of test driving and selecting their perfect ride. I think he was a bit disappointed when I explained to him that many people skip test drives altogether. They are so anxious to get the "deal done" that they forgo the full shopping experience and make decisions solely on what others tell them to do or buy (or both) or on car reviews they have read.

Ladies, cars are built to be test driven! So make a list of every make and model you want to drive. Just because you drive one and love it doesn't mean you should instantly stop there. Keep working your way down the list. Before making such a major purchase, I challenge you to get curious. Look at all the makes and models that fulfill your needs and desires from a new car, and then GO SHOPPING! Just as you would try on several new pair of shoes, you want to try on your new car!

I always recommend taking your first ride with the

salesperson driving the car—even if it's just around the block. That gives you a couple of minutes to get your bearings and see what he or she is doing to get the car set up. Drive a route that *you* want to drive. One of the oldest tricks in the book when it comes to test drives is that the dealerships have routes set up so that they can sell you based on specific features of the car.

Do not buy a car unless you have taken it out on the highway and accelerated the vehicle. And make sure that the second- and third-row seating is actually big enough for your tribe. I've seen so many people come back the next day and say, "I tried to put my car seats into the third seat, and it's just not big enough. I need a bigger vehicle." So make sure that you do all of those things during the test drive, and if it's a car that you think you really want, bring your car seats with you. Look in the trunk as well as in the back seat, and make sure you've got the space that you need. So many third-row seats eat up all of the trunk space.

Turn off the radio and all other distractions when you're taking a test drive. Something I was taught early on in my car career was to ask the customer what radio station they liked and then put the car on that radio station so that they could feel like it was already theirs. Don't do it! This is a business deal, and to make the best deal possible, we must keep emotion low and logic high. You're there to learn the features and feel of the car and see if it's something you want to spend the next two or three years driving. When you're out driving around with that salesperson, try not to show any emotion. You're there to act as the hunter. If you start saying, "Oh my God, I love this car!" you become the hunted.

Never engage in negotiations while on a test drive. Salespeople are trained to ask you "pre-closing questions" such as “Can you see yourself driving this car?” “Does this car work for you?” and “How does this car make you feel?” This is a business deal; treat it accordingly. First you buy the car, *then* you can tell everybody how much you love it.

FIERCE Girl's Car Buying Hack

When test driving, take the first spin with your salesperson, and then ask for fifteen minutes to take the car out alone. Roll down the windows, crank the stereo, and really take in the feel of the road. Pull over to the side of the road, take a selfie with the car, and send it to a few of your besties. *You* need to decide how the car makes you feel. Are you excited sitting behind the wheel? Does the driver's seat fit your body? Do you feel comfortable or intimidated driving in traffic? Does the car REALLY have enough power for you? Does it make the statement you want to make when you pull into the driveways of your friends and peers? Truly assessing these areas takes time, and it requires the opportunity to have some alone time to reflect on your thoughts and feelings. *Take that time!*

15

LEASING VERSUS BUYING/FINANCING

"You get in life what you have the courage to ask for."
—Oprah Winfrey

I feel compelled to reveal a secret to you: I have never leased a car. I don't have a good reason other than the fact that I tend to keep a car for a really long time. I still own the 1987 Nissan 300ZX I bought when it was brand new; my husband has had a blast restoring it. Now that you know that, I also want to clarify that I do believe in leasing cars—for the right reasons. My dealership was in Texas, where leasing is not quite as popular as it is in larger markets. It seems everything is much more spread out here, so it's easy to rack up the miles. In this chapter, I will explain to you the difference between financing and leasing your car.

FIERCE Girl's Car Buying Hack

Don't let someone talk you into leasing solely based on the lower payments it may offer. Leasing can be great, but it's not for everyone. Keep reading, and then *you* decide which option is right for you at any given point in time.

Financing a car requires that you take out an auto loan to help you purchase the vehicle, whereas leasing a car involves making monthly payments that allow you to use the car for a predetermined amount of time. When you finance a vehicle, you assume that you own it (assuming you make all of your payments).

Let's talk about the pros and cons of leasing a car. Here are some of the pros:

- No or low down payment
- Covered by a factory warranty
- Lower monthly payments
- No upfront sales tax fees

And here are some of the cons:

- Excess mileage penalties
- Fees for excessive wear and tear
- Early lease termination fees
- Generally higher insurance premiums

I'm frequently asked whether or not leasing a car is a good idea. Keep in mind that, if you're the girl who has to have a vehicle every three years simply because you don't really want to maintain or mess with the maintenance of a vehicle, leasing is the key. I believe that the biggest benefit of leasing a car rather than buying one is that you usually get more car for the money by leasing. A lease involves paying the depreciation on the car rather than the entire purchase price. Leasing also benefits drivers who don't have much money saved up for a down payment. You are actually driving the car during its most trouble-free years, when everything is new and under factory warranty.

Other frequently asked questions about leasing:

Q: Is it a good idea to buy the car at the end of the lease?

A: If the residual value is set low, you can buy the car for less than half of its worth at the end of the lease. Moreover, after the returned cars either directly or through an action, dealerships will often negotiate a buyout price that means more to you and allows you to avoid that hassle and expense. I recently helped a customer who had leased a Lexus GX 460. Her residual amount was $6,000 less than the value of the car. That meant that if she wanted to go and buy that same vehicle from a used car dealer, she would have paid $6,000 more for it. That was winning for sure. How do you get deals like this? It's not always easy, but keep an eye out for a low money factor. Money factor is a nice term for interest rate. You convert a money factor to a percentage by multiplying it by 2400. For example, if you are at a dealership and they tell you the money factor of the lease is .00256, the interest rate is actually 6.14 percent. So, the best thing to do when leasing a car is to make sure that you see the special lease rates or money factors. This will help get your payment low. Of course, you will also want to negotiate the price as well.

Q: I really want the lowest payment possible, is leasing a good option?

A: If you're looking to keep your monthly expenses low, a lease might be a good option for you. A typical car lease payment can be up to 60 percent lower than your monthly payments would be were you to purchase the same vehicle and finance it with a traditional auto loan.

Q: What are the benefits of leasing?

A: The biggest benefit of leasing is that it usually allows you to get a more expensive car with more features. You will still pay for maintenance (sometimes, it is included on luxury vehicles, so be sure to ask) and some repairs (tires, batteries, wiper blades, etc.). Your lease agreement will specifically state who is responsible for maintenance and repairs for the lease term. My friend, Brooke, will *only* lease cars. She is a powerhouse CEO with the ability to write a check for anything on the lot. When I questioned her about this, she said, "I don't care about the payments. I see cars as depreciating assets, so I let the manufacture take the hit up front." She does a "one-pay" lease. What that means is she sets up a twenty-four-month lease on the car she wants and writes the dealership a check upfront for all twenty-four payments. Since Mercedes is her car of choice, that typically means she only finances 40 percent of the car (due to high residual and short lease term). So, on a 120,000 Mercedes coupe, she's only "financing/leasing" $48,000 via a twenty-four month lease. She pays upfront, and she's cruising in style. Since she runs it through her company, it's also a tax write off. Remember, if you're self-employed, talk to your CPA about the most tax advantageous way to buy or lease a new car!

Q: Are there tax advantages to leasing?

A: According to Credit Karma, leasing a car if you're self-employed can have a different effect on your taxes. If you use your leased vehicle for your business, you may be able to deduct some or even all the vehicle's operating costs. This will depend on how much of the vehicle's use is for business purposes and how you deduct business expenses.

When you use your leased car for business, you can either use the standard mileage rate deduction or deduct actual expenses. To deduct all or part of your lease payment, you must use the actual expense method. You can only deduct the portion of your lease payments that is attributed to the business use of the vehicle. When you choose the actual expense method, you may also be able to deduct other vehicle-related costs, such as depreciation, maintenance, repairs, gas, insurance, and registration fees.

If you're leasing a car simply for personal use, the tax impact isn't much different from that of buying a car. Just be aware that there are rules on how businesses can deduct vehicle-related expenses, including the cost of a car lease. If you're not sure how to deduct business-related vehicle expenses, it might be a good idea to seek advice from a tax professional.

SHARON LECHTER'S THOUGHTS: LEASING VERSUS FINANCING

In Sharon's mind, there are six key factors to consider when exploring this decision.

Ownership

When you purchase/finance the car along with the bank that gives you the loan. Once you pay off the loan, the car is 100 percent yours.

When you lease a car, you are only renting it. You do not own it. When the lease is over, you have to return the car to the leasing agency.

Mileage

There are no mileage restrictions when you purchase a car, but when you lease one, the number of miles you can put on the car over the course of the lease is limited. If you exceed that number, you will have to pay a per-mile charge over the limit as described in your lease agreement.

Monthly Payments

Monthly payments are typically higher when you purchase/finance a car, however you own the car at the end of the loan term. When you lease a car, on the other hand, your payments are typically lower because you are only renting the vehicle. When you turn it in at the end of the lease, the leasing company can sell or re-lease it. If you choose to purchase the car at the end of your lease, your total cost will end up being more than if you had bought the car originally.

Wear and Tear

Wear and tear is not included in your loan cost when you purchase/finance a vehicle. However, when you lease you will be charged more at the end of the lease for anything they consider to be more than "normal wear and tear."

Insurance

The lender may require higher coverage than you want to carry when you purchase a vehicle. But the coverage is usually less expensive than it is for leased cars.

Car Envy Affordability

You need to be able to qualify to purchase the car of your dreams. However, you may be able to lease that car instead given the lower payments. *Be sure to check out the insurance cost first*, and remember that you will not own the car at the end of the lease term. Weighing these factors can help you determine if the lease option is still worth it.

16

ONE-PRICE DEALERSHIPS

"If you don't like the road you're walking, start paving another one."
—Dolly Parton

I have a firm opinion about one-price dealerships. That being said, one of my best friends, Stephanie, always goes to one to purchase her cars. She calls me every time she's in the market for car, which is quite often as she has four adult children for whom she furnishes cars. She trades about every eighteen months so in the fifteen years I have known her, she has purchased between 25 and 30 cars. Have you ever had a friend who calls you every time she needs your expertise but then she doesn't follow your advice? That's Steph. She always ends up at a one-price dealership. She always pays—in my opinion—$1,000 to $2,000 too much for her car, but she's always thrilled with the experience. So she always goes back.

Sounds counterintuitive right? She *knows* she's paying paying too much. She knows she could find a comparable car at a franchised dealer, and with the help of her car dealer friend, Lisa, get a smoking deal. So why doesn't she? In Stephanie's words, "I like the huge selection; I like that nobody hassles me; I like not negotiating back and forth; I like that my salesperson does the paperwork cradle-to-grave (meaning that the salesperson also handles the financing paperwork)." She likes that she can do the entire transaction 100 percent online and only needs to show up for delivery. She *loves* her approach to car shopping, and that's why she trades so often.

Are these sorts of dealerships lies of the devil? I believe that their transparency is increasing each year due to the plethora of car buying information one can find online. The dealer trend is actually to move toward a no-haggle sales process. While only a minority of dealers currently employ a no-haggle system, many have found that their profits actually increase after switching.

No-haggle dealerships are obviously attractive for car buyers who hate negotiating, but do they offer better prices? The short answer is no. The reason the American franchise system is strong is that it allows consumers—not dealers—to set the market prices. The reason I do what I do is to empower *all* consumers to make educated purchases while rewarding solid automotive retailers for doing business the right way. Within the one-price dealership model, there is no common pricing system among the many participating dealerships. Some price their cars as low as the market will bear while others factor in a comfortable profit. Some no-haggle dealers will not budge whatsoever on the price while others will go lower if presented with a better offer from another dealer.

The biggest problem for consumers who purchase at one-price dealerships is that the dealerships attempt to convey "transparency," but in actuality they are making their money somewhere. As you know, I am a believer in a fair profit for the dealer, but in my opinion, your best shot at the greatest savings comes with your ability to negate the price of the car. Many car shoppers assume that if the dealer is upfront in terms of the price of the car, they will also be upfront about other aspects, and this simply isn't true. Many times, there are all kinds of add-ons to the vehicle. No-haggle dealerships that sell a large volume of cars usually offer good prices, but I would never recommend choosing a dealership solely because they offer no-haggle prices. I recommend that you follow my step-by-step car buying process to get the best deal.

One of the things I most dislike about the one-price shopping model is the fact that the dealer franchise system is based on healthy competition. I truly believe that, as a consumer, it's best to be able to compare dealerships—not only from a pricing standpoint but from a sales and service perspective. If they have a hard and fast rule about not negotiating on the sales price of the vehicle, they're making their money elsewhere. They must in order to stay in business. So, they're either not paying you the same amount for your trade-in or they're charging you a greater number of fees in the finance department or they've added on a bunch of features to the car that you really don't need.

17

TIMING IS EVERYTHING

"Don't stop until you're proud."
—Unknown

Did you know that you can save money by properly timing the purchase of your car? Dealerships and salespeople are pressured to sell more vehicles during certain periods, so catching them during these times will give you maximum negotiating power. For example, each dealership has monthly sales goals, and manufacturers often offer bonuses for the sale of specific vehicles. If a dealer intends to sell above a certain threshold, when it comes down to the final days of the month, the pressure is on to meet quotas. Therefore, the final few days of each month present a great car buying opportunity for you.

People often wonder whether they should buy a car at the end of the model year? The answer is, it really depends. Can you get a better deal? Absolutely. But if the model or vehicle is changing body styles, I don't advise doing it. I don't care how much money you're saving, because you're buying a car that's becoming obsolete. So be very careful at the end of the year. By waiting until year end, you also risk the opportunity to have a great selection of cars from which to choose. I recommend asking for the price on the model year end as well as the price on the bran-new model year. You might find that there's not that much difference, and if that's the case, I definitely recommend purchasing or leasing the newer model year.

Another hot topic from my tribe revolves around whether or not it's a good idea to buy a demo. Every once in a while, you may come across a great deal on a demo. These are new cars that have been driven by the employees, family members, or service customers of the dealership for a few months. They usually have between 2,000 and 6,000 miles on the odometer, and they are not considered used because the car has never been sold or titled.

They're legally considered to be new, so they qualify for all the rebates, special financing, and new car warranty. Demos should be priced lower than a comparable new car (but they aren't always), and at first glance often seem to be a really good deal. That said, there are a few things you need to watch for:

The Warranty

Although demos are covered by the original manufacturer's warranty, just like any new car, you need to realize that the warranty starts at mile zero. If the car comes with a three year, thirty-six-mile bumper-to-bumper warranty, the demo unit (which already has 10,000 miles on the odometer) has already used up a good chunk of the mileage that would make it qualify for the warranty. You might be thinking, "Well, if I don't put a lot of miles on a car, I'm still covered for three years." This could actually be a problem as well, as warranty coverage begins when the dealer establishes a service date on the vehicle. The dealer might have already placed the vehicle in service, so you need to find out whether or not they have and what kind of service they have performed. The warranty date reflects the day the new car warranty was put into effect, and if someone has been driving it already for three months, they've already used up that portion of the warranty.

What You Should Pay for a Demo

A good way to figure out what you should pay is to see what a comparable new car is selling for. In general, you want a discount of twenty-five to forty cents per mile driven on a vehicle that's been driven at least 5,000 miles. This equates to a discount between $1,250 and $2,000. Realize that demo vehicles are not always great deals and, in fact, most experts recommend against buying them. Sometimes, however, there are extra discounts provided by the dealer-manufacturer for demo vehicles, so if you come across an exceptional deal, just be sure to pay attention to the warranty and the overall condition of car before agreeing to the purchase.

FIERCE Girl's Car Buying Hack

Ask the salesperson if the owner or General Manager has any of their personal demos for sale. They usually take a little better care of them than would someone from the general public. One thing I know for sure is that they have them cleaned up and maintained at all times. Beware of factory/manufacturer demos. They are from the auction and driven by manufacturer field reps or used at car shows for display (which means that four million or so people have crawled through them!).

18

NEGOTIATING THE DEAL

"If you obey all the rules, you miss all the fun."
—Katherine Hepburn

Now we get to the juicy part. How do you negotiate the best possible deal? Most car shoppers do this very much the wrong way. They think negotiating face-to-face with a car salesman is the way to go. Never set foot in a dealership when negotiating. In short: *don't negotiate*. That's right. It likely sounds counterintuitive, but the way to get the best deal on a new or used car is to follow this simple direction: Get pricing via email only. That's really all there is to it. It is a matter of following directions and gathering prices rather than actually negotiating (which sounds so much more civilized, doesn't it?).

A few of my other award-winning strategies:

- Always negotiate everything separately. Dealers love to combine your trade-in with the price of a new car and payment. This creates price confusion and it makes it hard to compare deals. The same goes for financing or add-ons such as extended warranties. Shop around for the best deals and ***never negotiate*** based on monthly payments or down payment.

- If you've come to the dealership completely armed with a pre-negotiated offer and a preset appointment, you're not going to have to get into all of the back-and-forth haggling that female consumers hate! The best way to do what I am recommending is to deal with the dealership's internet department. That way, you never have to deal with that man or woman behind the curtain and spend hours going back and forth!
- If you have set up everything ahead of time and the deal changes as soon as you get to the dealership, that is your cue that these are not your people and you need to get up and walk out of the dealership. Do not play the back-and-forth game. It's 2019 after all.
- When negotiating a car deal, it's smart to know which items are *not* negotiable. Many consumers try to negotiate fees that a dealer has no control over. This frustrates salespeople and demonstrates your lack of car-buying knowledge. If there's a certain fee you're not happy with, it's best to try to lower the overall price instead of focusing on that specific fee. Here are some examples of non-negotiable fees: sales tax, tag and title, registration fees, documentation fees (although doc fees may differ from dealer to dealer, they're not allowed to charge different

> rates for different customers. So they're non-negotiable. Many states, such as New York and New Jersey, set the rates on doc fees, while other states allow dealers to charge up to a certain amount, sometimes as high as $1,000), lease acquisition disposition and mileage fees. If you're leasing a vehicle, the leasing company, which is usually not the dealer, will charge an acquisition or disposition fee. Since the dealer has no control over this, it's a non-negotiable fee. Same goes for mileage overage fees. If you feel like you're driving the car more than the allotted miles, prepay the overages.

When we're negotiating, why don't we talk about the incentives that are offered by the manufacturers? Incentives are a way for manufacturers to help sell slower-moving vehicles. Most people are familiar with cash back incentives, whereby you get a manufacturer discount when buying a specific mode. They typically range between $500 and $5,000, but there are all kinds of bonus cash lease deals, financing incentives, and loyalty programs available. It's tough to keep up with all of them, but most people don't know that manufacturers also give additional marketing incentives to dealers. These are usually available on leftover models or models that are selling poorly.

Incentives are great when you're buying a new car, but they also come with a downside. Too many incentives will lead to a drop in resale value. Some manufacturers will limit incentives, and usually, the manufacturers who will limit incentives have vehicles that don't depreciate as quickly.

While we're discussing negotiating, we have to talk about budget. Today's average new car sells for about

$30,000, and that's before factoring in taxes, fees, insurance, and other expenses. I know it's boring to talk about budgeting, but you really need to do this before you start shopping. Most people overestimate how much they can afford, which leads to uncomfortably high payments. Buying a car should be a great experience, not one that makes you worry about your finances month after month. Those who need a car loan should follow these guidelines:

- Your monthly payment should be no more than 15 percent of your take-home pay (after taxes).
- Limit your car loans to sixty (60) months or less.
- The down payment should be at least 20 percent of the purchase price.

If you can't hit these budget targets, you need to consider buying a lower-priced car. It's much better to be safe than sorry when you're budgeting for a new car. The purpose of this book isn't to help you choose a car. There are lots of websites that do a good job with that. My mission is to help you save money and be the best negotiator you can be so that you're an empowered consumer. That's why Cars Her Way was created to begin with!

It doesn't matter to me which car you choose; I want to help you get the best deal regardless. If you buy an expensive car that depreciates slowly, it may end up costing you less over the long term than if you purchase a lower-priced vehicle that loses its value quickly. Depreciation makes up the bulk of a vehicle's cost, so you need to pay close attention to this factor. If you choose a $30,000 car, you essentially have a depreciating asset. You can sell your car at any time and get some money back, but the depreciation is your actual cost. Luxury vehicles, in particular, tend to depreciate most quickly. If you have your heart set on a luxury vehicle, it makes sense to purchase a used model or consider leasing it. It will save you thousands of dollars in depreciation.

A willingness to be flexible about your vehicle choices allows you to shop for the best deals. Many shoppers have their hearts set on one specific model and refuse to drive the competition. This is a huge mistake. One of the best pieces of advice I can give you is, go out and test drive as many competing vehicles as you can. I promise you'll be surprised by the results and like cars you never thought you would. Once you're behind the wheel, options that were a no-go previously will suddenly become attractive, while others that you thought were awesome will turn out to be only mediocre. Don't trust only the reviews you find online. Everyone has their own opinion when it comes to cars, and most car sites and magazines are geared toward auto enthusiasts, those who are more interested in performance than driving and reliability.

19

OFF TO THE FINANCE OFFICE

"Stress does not go with my outfit."
—Unknown

In the interest of full transparency, I spent almost ten years of my automotive career as a finance director. That means that my job was to sell the loans to the banks, contract with and do all paperwork for the customers, and sell extended warranties and other add-on items. I'm going to give you my take on all of those items because I believe in them. Unlike other automotive experts, I sat in this seat (literally) and actually saw the benefits of such options for the majority of our customers. I watched claims being paid out that otherwise could have spelled financial disaster for my clients.

In marketing, it's a well-known fact that consumers are easier to up-sell after they've agreed to buy something. An additional $1,000 in vehicle cost will increase the monthly payment by less than $20 on a sixty-month loan. It doesn't seem like much, but it quickly adds up, and there are all kinds of add ons available. Dealers will try to sell products such as:

- Prepaid maintenance plans
- Paint fabric protection
- Rust proofing
- Window etching
- Tire sealants
- Road hazard insurance
- Extended warranties
- Gap insurance

The list goes on. There are many add-ons that I consider worth having, including extended warranties, gap insurance, maintenance, and tire and wheel warranties.

Let's talk about extended warranties. If you plan on keeping your vehicle for many years and don't want to worry about repair bills, it's usually a good idea to invest in an extended warranty. I invest in an extended warranties for every vehicle I purchase and I recommend to my family and friends that they do the same. Extended warranties take over after the manufacturer warranty expires, usually after three years or 36,000 miles. They cover pretty much everything except normal wear and tear items such as oil changes, brake pads, batteries, blades, and tires. You can usually purchase an extended warranty on a new vehicle as long as you are within one month or 1,000 miles of manufacturer's warranty expiration. If you miss this deadline, you can still buy an extended warranty, but you'll be charged based off of used car prices, which is quite a bit more expensive. There's usually a lot of negotiating room when it comes to extended warranties. My recommendation is to always purchase one that is manufacturer-backed, if it's available. It will be more expensive but worth the additional cost.

Gap insurance is also recommended. When you take out a loan to buy a new car, chances are, you will owe more than the car's worth for some time. The reason for that is simple: new cars depreciate very quickly. In fact, the loan payments may not even make up for the depreciation loss during the first half of your loan term. It all depends on the amount of your down payment, length of your loan term, and rate of depreciation of your particular car. If your new car were to be stolen or totaled via accident or fire, your insurance will cover only the value of the car at the time of loss. If you owe more on the loan than the vehicle was worth, you won't have to pay out-of-pocket as long as you have gap insurance. In some cases, this gap could be as high as several thousand dollars. Gap insurance will pay off the difference, including any deductible required by your car insurance company. Gap insurance is especially useful in cases where the traded-in car was upside down on the loan, meaning that you owed more than it was worth and you're financing the difference within your payments on the new car. If, on the other hand, you make a down payment of at least 20 percent on your new vehicle, you won't need gap insurance. Gap Insurance policies sell for between $300 and $700 and can be purchased through a dealer or your current car insurance company. If you do intend on getting it, make sure to shop around.

Since we're discussing the finance office, let's discuss circumstances where your credit is perhaps not particularly fantastic. Maybe you went through a divorce or something devastating happened, and you're now working to repair your credit. The reason it's important to discuss this is that those with bad credit are often at the greatest risk of being ripped off when it comes to acquiring a car loan.

Getting a loan when you have poor credit is difficult, especially in this economy. Most lenders will require that you have at least two years of steady employment and residence. They'll also require that you come up with a comparatively large down payment. Given my extensive experience, I believe that the best way to get a loan with bad credit is to identify a co-signer, usually a parent or close relative. This person will agree to make the car payments for you if you fail to do so. If you end up qualifying for a car loan with a high interest rate, you can always try to refinance it a year or two later. Having made your payments on time should have helped to improve your credit score, which will qualify you for a better rate. If you have negative equity (meaning that you owe more on the car than it's currently worth), the best thing you can do is to keep making payments until you have paid off the car. If you really need a new car, you should pay off the negative equity whenever you sell or trade in the car. If you don't have the cash to do so, I suggest that you try to find a car that has a higher dealer incentive or rebate, which could help pay off the negative equity. A big mistake is rolling too much negative equity into your new car loan. You'll just end up digging yourself deeper into the hole, eventually landing you in an undesirable position.

Let's talk about first-time buyer and college grad programs, special finance programs for first-time buyers and college graduations, which I really like. Look for those that are sponsored by car manufacturers. Ford, in particular, has a good one that provides loans to first-time buyers with a stable employment history and a certain income level. Toyota, Nissan, Honda, and KIA are among those that provide special rebates for college grads. Contact your local dealers to find out if you qualify for these programs. Also, if you're new to the credit market, check out your credit union, which is another great lending source for first-time home or car buyers. Many credit unions will work with borrowers who have little-to-no credit history. If you're already a member of a credit union (and they're pretty easy to join), you may find that none of these options works for you, in which case you'll need to look for a lower price used vehicle while you save up enough money to purchase it outright. In the meantime, start building your credit by using a credit card and paying your bills on time each month. Establishing solid credit is a long-term process, but it will come in handy in the future.

SHARON LECHTER'S FINANCE OFFICE ADVICE

"When you are serious about buying the car and ready to secure your financing, you will want to do a more thorough analysis of your financing options. Do your homework ahead of time and compare the various loans available before you have the finance office start pulling your credit report. You may find that you are able to get pre-approved by a bank at a better rate than the dealership is offering. The following chart will help you compare various options. This analysis should help you make the best decision on which financing is best for you and your personal financial situation."

Amount of Loan $ ___________

FINANCIAL INSTITUTION COMPARISON

	Bank #1	Bank #2	Bank #3
APR	______	______	______
Length of Loan	______	______	______
Monthly Payment	______	______	______
Total Finance Charge	______	______	______
Total To Be Repaid	______	______	______

Loan Approval or Rejection

"Once you have made your decision as to what car you want, you will need to complete your loan application," notes Lechter. "You may be asked to sign permission letters to allow the lender to send verifications of employment and deposits to your employer and financial institutions. If there are any blemishes on your credit report, you may want to address them and provide the documents that you have gathered to help the lender get past them.

"If your loan is approved, make sure all the information is correct on the final loan documents including your monthly payments—ensure that they are the amount you agreed to pay.

"If your loan is rejected, ask why. Get a copy of the credit report they used and work hard to fix and improve your credit history so that the next time you apply you will be accepted instead of being tempted to look for loans with extremely high interest rates."

Know Your Consumer Rights

Here is a bit more great advice from Sharon Lechter (the woman knows her stuff!).

"The FTC enforces the Equal Credit Opportunity Act, which does not allow you to be discriminated against or treated differently because of your race, religion, national origin, sex, marital status, age, or because you get public assistance. Not everyone who applies for credit gets it or gets the same terms: factors like income, expenses, debts, and credit history are among the considerations lenders use to determine your creditworthiness.

"If, during the process of purchasing your car or applying for any type of loan, you feel that you have been discriminated against, you can file a complaint. To file a complaint or to get free information on consumer issues, visit www.ftc.gov or call toll-free 1-877-FTC-HELP (1-877-382-4357).

20

THE FINALE: THE DELIVERY OF YOUR NEW CAR

"A wise girl knows her limits. A smart girl knows she has none."

—Marilyn Monroe

You've proven it. You're a great consumer, and you've gotten a great deal. So now let's talk about the delivery of your vehicle. After all, you've spent a good portion of your day at the dealership, negotiated the price of your new car, negotiated the value of your trade, and set up financing. But the most important part is the delivery. How many times have you gotten home and wondered, "How do I work the GPS?" Or, "How do I turn on the windshield wipers?" I highly recommend setting up time on a different day to come back to the dealership and complete the delivery process, during which everything in your car is set up for you.

You've received first class delivery of your car. You've also finished the paperwork in the business office. I know you're ready to go, but you still need to spend some time walking around your car and ensuring that it is clean and undamaged. Be sure to inspect open the trunk and make sure the spare tire is in place. If there is one, go to the hood and have your salesperson quickly point out hotspots such as the battery. You need to make sure that you know where all the controls are located as well as how things such as headlights, windshield wipers, heat, air conditioning, and navigation operate. I know you'll be eager to get out of the dealership ASAP, which is why, many times, it's good to schedule another appointment to come back and get a new vehicle orientation. Make sure you feel comfortable in the vehicle before you drive away.

Also ensure that you have been provided with all relevant documents such as insurance and vehicle registration, financing documents, the owner manual and a second set of keys. Be patient, and recognize that minor delays are sometimes unavoidable. If you find anything not up to your expectations, simply note it on a piece of paper and bring it to the attention of the staff. Your aim is to rectify any faults, not create an unpleasant scene during what should be a joyous occasion.

Be sure to inspect your vehicle in the daylight and in an open space. Take your time and note even the smallest imperfections. It is very difficult to justify scratches and minor dents after you leave the dealership.

Your Delivery checklist

- Check all doors for dings and scratches.
- Check the hood and the trunk to ensure they open and shut properly and that all rubber linings are soft.

- Check the windshields for any cracks, scratches, or spots that may be difficult to remove later.
- Check the interior of the car, and be on the lookout for any kind of soil on the seats, upholstery, or carpet. Also, make sure all cloth and leather is intact.
- Ensure there are no warning lights flashing on the instrument cluster panel
- Ensure that the fuel level is adequate and the engine temperature is within the correct range
- Ensure that you have all the floor mats and the spare tire if either or both were part of the package.
- Make sure you have the second set of keys and warranty books
- Note the mileage on the vehicle at the time of final delivery. Typically, anything below 100 miles is acceptable, though it will vary depending on how your vehicle was delivered from the manufacturer's yard, how many test drives it's been on, and any service inspections and/or road-ready tests it's undergone.

21

LET'S HEAR IT FOR THE GUYS

"A man with dreams needs a woman with vision."
—*Unknown*

Working in a male-dominated field has had its fair share of positive moments. In an industry that has such a "bad wrap," there are truly some incredible men who believe women have value, understand their daily struggle, and support them. I am blessed to call both Glenn Lundy and Jim Wilkinson dear friends. I am grateful to know them, and they have supported me both personally and professionally over the years.

Jim, the General Sales Manager of Fred Haas Toyota World in Houston, TX, a truly amazing. He told me the following story about his mom's influence on his life when I interviewed him on my podcast, Big Sellers:

For as long as I can remember, my mom has been my greatest influence. I could not imagine who I would be if it weren't for the early life lessons learned as the proud, eldest son of a hardworking single mom. Growing up, my mother filled roles of both Mom and Dad, which was no easy task with a hard-headed, thrill-seeking young son.

I find it ironic that I'm the sales director at the largest dealership in Gulf States Toyota, because during most of my youth, we never owned a car. To this day, my mom doesn't drive. Growing up in New Orleans, we moved a lot to be near bus and streetcar routes. My mom worked multiple jobs and continually strived to improve our situation, but each new opportunity meant a new change for the family. Every move meant being the new kid at a new school. She taught me early not to feel like an outsider by adapting to my surroundings while holding firm to my identity. My mom, to this day, preaches, "Stay true to yourself in the face of adversity." She stressed that in an ever-changing world, the only constant is you. My mom instilled in me that work ethic is everything, always imploring us not to lower the bar but rise to the challenge. I never knew we were poor. I never felt poor. At times, my mom had part-time jobs as well as a full-time job. She worked hard to insulate us from that hardship and always ensured that we were grounded, not materialistic. Variety proved to be the spice of our life. Our limitations birthed resourcefulness and forged my creativity.

My upbringing and my mom's influence have greatly influenced my practices as a businessman. I've always been conscious of opening doors to success by understanding and supporting the challenges faced by today's single mother. When I recruit, I look for specific traits that reflect those exemplified by my mom: the ability to adapt, the determination to overcome obstacles, and the tenacity to succeed against all odds. I've found that women continue to demonstrate all of these qualities exceptionally well. Not only that, but by paying attention to my female colleagues, I continue to learn new lessons and expand my understanding of what it means to excel in a challenging world.

It is my honor to use my privilege and community standing to aid and amplify these voices in our industry. My mother taught me not to wait for a moment that might not come, but to forge opportunity where others saw adversity. The women I have had the pleasure of working with have attacked the challenges of this industry with unprecedented passion. I advocate for them and guide when necessary, but largely step out of the way and simply take notes.

Glenn Lundy, who I also introduced at the beginning of the chapter, was the General Manager of one of the largest dealerships in the USA. Glenn and I were introduced by a mutual business acquaintance and became fast friends. We have the same belief system when it comes to dealership culture and the way a dealership needs to operate.

Glenn is the father to seven beautiful children and is married to an amazing woman, Leslie. He has since left his high-profile job and now leads over 35,000 people in his private group and morning podcast, #RiseandGrind. He shared a story with me about a young woman named Ericka who he hired against all odds. I have since gotten to know Ericka, and she's a powerhouse. Glenn tells Ericka's story beautifully:

There were 267 new units sold, 585 pre-owned units sold,

and we still had a few days left in the month. Things were going well, but I needed more sales people. One of the hardest parts about running the second largest used car volume franchise dealer in the country was keeping up with the staffing demands. It wasn't like our local people pool was much of an option. Being in a town of only 9,600, finding someone with enthusiasm, personality, a strong work ethic, professionalism, and good character was always a bit of a chore.

As I sat in my office, diligently reviewing our numbers, she walked in. She looked nervous and timid, yet had a unique light about her. She sat down and introduced herself as Ericka, and though she had never sold a car before in her life, she wanted the opportunity to come sell cars for me. The dealership I ran had grown massively over the previous seven years. Starting off as a small-town store selling no more than 150 cars a month, we had grown to the point where we were selling between 800 and 900 cars a month, with a record 1,000-car month on the books just prior to Ericka's arrival. The dealership had become a melting pot of personalities, ethnicities, age ranges, and experience sets, but one thing it still lacked was a solid selection of female salespeople.

That wasn't due to a male preference. It wasn't due to a lack of women in the area, and it had everything to do with the stigma that auto industry sales is a man's game. If you have ten applicants walk in the door, nine of them will be male. The industry simply has never focused on attracting powerful, intelligent, hard-working women, and therefore, the results are what they are.

Here Ericka was, staring at me intently, yet shyly, keeping eye contact—although forcibly, as though her instincts were telling her to turn and run, but she had chosen to fight instead. She came here for a reason and she was determined to follow through.

We chatted lightly at first, and Ericka expressed her desire to change her life. She had grown up around cars with a brother and dad who were racers, and she clearly knew how to turn a wrench. She had most recently been a hairstylist, had two kids and a boyfriend, and was struggling to make ends meet. She had been told a few times about a *big* dealership in a *small* town that was doing really well. She understood that everyone who worked there seemed to be making great money and enjoying life. To her, it sounded like a utopia, an oasis in a cold dark world, the complete opposite of the stereotype that came to mind when she thought of a car salesperson.

I asked the same question that I had asked many applicants before her: "How does your background check look? Any major crimes I need to know about?"

To my surprise, Ericka whipped out a copy of her background report and began to tell me an amazing story of addiction, criminality, and depression. I was shocked, floored really, but not by her past and her crimes—by her preparation and willingness to share so openly. She had embraced her past and moved on from it. She was not allowing herself to be defined by it. She even went so far as to tell me she could have legally had the items on her report removed, but she keeps them on there as a constant reminder of where she used to be, and the life to which she refuses to return.

After doing some research and the thought of a better life consuming her every waking moment, Ericka's "Momma" mode kicked in, and she knew she had to do something if she was going to give her kids the life they deserved. So, against the nay-saying words of her husband, there she sat in front of me.

I loved her story. I loved her fight. And I was sold immediately. I have always been a fan of hiring those with desire and drive over resumes and accolades. Show me a car salesman with twenty years under his belt and a handful of Salesman of the Month plaques, and I will show you a rug that's been beaten to death. I got results out of those whose desperation to win superseded their lack of experience. The only other piece of the puzzle for me is a person's character. All talent and no character does absolutely nothing for me; great character and small talent I can work with.

I won't go deeper into Ericka's story. What I will do, however, I'll share with you her amazing transformation as a sales woman who had never before sold a car, at the second largest used car franchise in the country, surrounded by absolute pros with many, many years in the business.

She killed it.

I mean, she absolutely killed it.

Within sixty days, she was one of the top five salespeople month-in and month-out, and since then she's consistently remained at or around number two on the board. She is relentless.

Her work ethic is second to none, her charm and charisma are contagious, her overwhelming desire to help others is apparent, and her ability to not give a rat's tail what other people say or do around her is admirable. She studied daily, trained harder than anyone, applied every strategy I developed, and did it all with an enormous smile on her face and a deep-seated appreciation for the opportunity.

She is selling cars with a chip on her shoulder and a purpose in her heart, and she makes that clear through her own website, GirlsDoCarsBetter.com (shameless plug for this amazing young woman).

And the kicker...I agree with her beliefs. I, too, believe there is a massive void of women that needs to be filled in automotive. Ericka is but one of many stories I have of women who stepped into my dealership nervous and feeble, but dominated in a short period of time. There's also Brenna, who went from receptionist to the number one finance person in the state in a matter of two years. And Julia, who made her way from the accounting office to top salesperson and, ultimately, a sub-prime finance manager. I could tell you about Brandy, or Mindy, or Lauren, who have all built amazing careers in the automotive industry. Instead I will simply tell you this:

Automobile purchases are primarily determined by the number one influencer in the world: WOMEN.

The fact that our industry still isn't hip to that fact is beyond me. Women hold all the cards, and yet our marketing, our showrooms, and our training are still focused on (and run by) men. It's both a travesty and an opportunity. If we can wrap our brains around this fact, we can begin to create change. If we can begin to create environments that serve our fierce women, we can attract more of them. And if we can educate more young women on the idea that, while being a hairstylist or a server or a receptionist is great if that's their passion, there are other areas in the marketplace where they can not only win but dominate.

FIERCE Girl's Business Tip

If you're looking for an exciting career that is fast-paced, if you love people and want to make some real money, consider the automotive industry. Our Trusted Dealer Partners are always hiring amazing people. www.carsherway.com. I must warn you, however, that if you don't love people, you'll want to find a different line of work!

22

FIERCE WOMEN CAN COLLECTIVELY CHANGE THE WORLD

"It's about women helping women and women doing things together and supporting each other."
—Diana Burch

This chapter is especially fun for me to write. I know this book is, as a whole, a girl's roadmap to cay buying, but I want to introduce you to the other side of the automotive industry— the fun and fast side. My friend, Diane Caplan, has had a long and very successful automotive career. We sat down over dinner a couple weeks prior to the publishing of this book, and I intended to make a very large ask of her. As one of the fifty most influential women in Houston, Texas, I wanted her to serve as an advisor to Cars Her Way. When you're building a movement, it requires collaboration and buy-in.

CHW's first market was Houston. It's the fourth largest city in the USA, so where better to start? I quickly sought out Diane, an all-around fabulous, badass automotive expert and founder of Heels & Horsepower. She's well respected in both the Houston luxury market as well as around the country. She is beautiful, and rolled up in her Bentley wearing head-to-toe couture. *Yes*, I thought, *this is a woman I need to know better!*

I asked her all the questions you would ask a prospective board member. Most importantly, I asked her if she would serve. If she would take on a highly visible leadership role to help empower *all* women consumers, not only in Houston but also around the country. I was ecstatic when she said, "Yes!"

Diane's amazing story started with a little girl and a '68 Ford Mustang in Deer Park, Texas. Growing up, Diane had more Matchbox Cars than Barbie Dolls. Knowing her today, you would never believe this fashion-loving, Chanel and Louboutin hoarder genuinely was—and a huge tomboy. To Diane, cars were more than just a vehicle that got one from point A to point B; they were an extension of the person behind the wheel. The start of her long chain of car ownership was a 1979 Camaro with a V8 engine, and she quickly flipped in and out of sports cars, from Mazda RX7s to Ford Mustangs.

But Diane's life changed forever when she finally got behind the wheel of her very first Mercedes-Benz.

A bright red CLK430, it was one of the very first red versions to hit the Houston streets. It wasn't so much the car that changed her life—it was the job opportunity that came with it: the chance to become a salesperson at a Mercedes-Benz dealership that was launching their new Internet Sales Department. Back then, salespeople didn't even have computers on their desks, and the entire online car buying concept was still new. With Diane's computer and website background, she took a chance and never looked back. It turned out to be the best decision she ever made.

However, the road wasn't easy—it never is in a male-dominated industry. But hard work, perseverance, and her passion for cars kept her going and quickly moved her up the ranks to management. Overseeing the eCommerce and Marketing areas for several large dealer groups, one of the highlights of Diane's role was producing car events and representing her dealers at various morning meetups around town.

Fast forward to 2017, when with over twenty years of luxury automotive experience behind her, Diane's new marketing company, BrightCatch Media, was working with brands such as Bentley, Rolls-Royce, Bugatti, Porsche, and Ferrari. Having watched the luxury and exotic car market grow year after year, Diane began seeing more and more women owning these car brands. She began thinking about how many ladies she knew in Houston who drove a Ferrari or Porsche and realized she knew at least ten right off the bat. She figured that if *she* knew ten ladies driving these luxury brands, *they* must each know ten ladies as well, and she could therefore quickly put together a women-only car show. Hence, Heels & Horsepower was born.

The first event drew approximately thirty ladies and their exotic or ultra-luxury cars. It attracted women from Austin, Dallas, and Houston. What started with what was intended to be a one-time event quickly turned into a bonafide car club with smaller events scheduled throughout the year and women joining monthly.

Now a registered trademark, Heels & Horsepower has big goals to expand the car empowerment message to women across the nation including hosting the world's largest ladies-only car show and track event in 2020 in partnership with Christina Nielsen's Accelerating Change mission.

The biggest and best reward for Diane has been the members Heels & Horsepower has cultivated. With their love of cars serving as their common bond, members are all very strong-minded in their own rights. Some are married, some are not; some are mothers, some not. Some members have husbands who are into cars, and some do not. As they've forged friendships with one another outside of the Heels & Horsepower events, the surge in women supporting other women has been the best thing to come out of Heels & Horsepower.

Diane's original goal continues to empower women through her message that it is okay for them to love cars. It is okay to buy the Porsche with the sport exhaust because you love the loud *purrrr* it makes when you turn the key in the ignition. It's totally cool that you track your McLaren or want to put a carbon fiber kit on your Ferrari. It's completely normal to want that manual transmission over the paddle shifters because you love to *feel* the car while you're blazing down the street. And yes, ladies, it is okay to enjoy the feeling you get when you are sitting at the stop light in your Lamborghini and a guy rolls up expecting to see a man behind the wheel—then does a double take when he sees a woman.

Exotic and ultra-luxury cars are for anyone who aspires to own and drive one. And now more than ever, they are owned and driven by women!

I am privileged to know many powerful women in the automotive industry and beyond, but one woman's story literally had me weeping. I met Evelyn Chatel in 2016 when she was a keynote speaker at the Women in Automotive annual conference.

When this beautiful, well-dressed woman took the stage, I had never before met her or even heard of her. Everything about her drew me in. Her quiet power, her carefully chosen words, her unapologetic belief in God and country. It was love at first sight for me. As I listened to her powerful story, I told myself that she and I needed to be friends.

She opened up with, "On March 17, 1967, at four years old, I stepped off the last Freedom Flight from Cuba. It was my mother, my brother, and me. My father had been detained in Cuba while trying to get food for our family. As we waited for him at the airport, my mother had no idea he had been arrested. The flight was boarding and my mother had to decide, *Do we stay in Cuba or board the last Freedom Flight to ever leave Cuba?*" She made a very scary and definite decision. Her decision was to escape communist Cuba.

What Evelyn's mother did not know as she boarded that Freedom Flight with her two young children was that she was pregnant with her third child. She had no money, very few personal belongings, and two small children when she made the decision that day to bring her family to a free country. It ended up being an absolute Godsend that she was pregnant because Evelyn's sister was born a US citizen, and because of that, her father was allowed out of exile and was deported to the US to be reunited with his family.

I looked around the room of that event, and there was not a dry eye in the place. Evelyn's delivery and transparency about her childhood and plight as an immigrant were so beautiful. She told us about the way her mother worked multiple jobs as a seamstress to support her two children and the fact that they didn't even realize they were poor. She spoke with such admiration for her mother and her struggle to keep the family together as they waited for their father to be released from the Cuban jail.

I wondered why I had never heard of this woman before, but after hearing her full story, it became clear. She isn't about fame or being the center of attention. She's about her family, her employees, and her faith in God.

Evelyn's automotive career started in 1981 when she was eighteen years old, as a greeter at Courtesy Ford. She learned very quickly that she had a passion for people. That passion she still exists today in all that she does. She worked her way from greeter to cashier, service writer, and eventually Director of Fixed Operations. I must point out she was most likely the *only* Fixed Operations Director in her region, and her responsibilities included managing the service department, service advisors, mechanics, technicians, and parts department—a huge responsibility for anyone, and a very unlikely job for a woman in those years.

From the Fixed Operations Director, she was promoted to General manager in 1996 (another huge jump uncommon if not unheard of for women). In 2005, she became the Owner/Partner of Freedom Auto Group in Harrisburg, Pennsylvania.

Clearly, this is a woman who overcame all odds. When I sat own with her in advance of writing this book I asked her a few questions:

Q: What is the number one reason you believe you have been successful against all odds as both an immigrant and a woman in a male-dominated field?

. . .

A: "Not understanding the word No. When you grow up like I did, with all the odds stacked against you, you understand fight or flight. I believe growing up in survival mode is the best formal business training anyone could possibly have.

Q: What is the biggest obstacle you faced in a male-dominated industry?

A: As a woman, trying to balance my responsibility as a leader, a wife, and a mother.

Q: How did you balance all three of those incredibly important roles?

A: (laughs) Balance is a lie we tell ourselves There is NO work life balance. I spent many years feeling guilty I sacrificed my kids plays, ball games, and family reunions to live up to what I thought I needed to do as a leader. My husband, Jerry, and I agreed that we could not have children or any other major life event any time at the end of the month. It was a pact we made. Talk about having to be well organized!

Q: Do you have any regrets about the choices you made?

A: Regrets? No. But looking back, I know I wasted valuable

time not being present, feeling like I was never enough. Not enough at home, not enough at work, not enough with my friends. That's a huge burden that I know many women bear.

Q: Lastly, what piece of advice you would give your younger self?

A: Don't try to balance. It doesn't exist. You need to give your time and attention to what is pulling on you at that minute. It might be your employee, it might be your children. Just go with it. It's all you can do. Never have regrets.

I am so honored that when I made the prediction in 2016 that Evelyn and I would be friends. It came true, and I consider her a dear friend and confidant. We share many similar experiences from the automotive industry, and we are trusted advisors to one another.

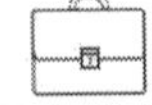

FIERCE Girl's Business Tip

Be intentional about meeting other amazing people at your company and within your industry. There is so much knowledge to absorb and camaraderie to be had. If I hadn't made the decision that I was going to make Evelyn Chatel my friend, I would have missed out on so much! She is so important to me, as both a friend and a trusted colleague.

We were not put in this world to go it alone. As women, we are relationship driven. I believe that fear of rejection often holds us back from forming strategic alliances that can build us up in both business and life. Feel the fear, and reach out anyway.

23

BUILD A MOVEMENT, CHANGE THE WORLD

"I always believed that one woman's success can only help another woman's success."
—Gloria Vanderbilt

My story began in the automobile industry, but that is not where it will end. Unleashing my ideas on the world will allow me to show everyone how to find success—however they define it.

How many relationships and opportunities have passed you by because didn't grab the moment? Stop. Stop all of it. Stop waiting for the stars and planets to align. Stop spinning your wheels with approaches that may or may not work for you. Stop hoping that *something* will click. Take control of your narrative and harness your power.

Commit to crushing mediocrity dead in its tracks. By purposefully and strategically abandoning your many rivals as well as your own doubts, you will be able to forge your own path to the finish line. It won't be easy, but the key lies in being willing to write your own narrative and redefine the very idea of success *for you*. Forging mutual alliances will build you up with others for life, putting you in control for the long-term.

It's my sincere hope that *Car Buying, Her Way* has empowered you to be an educated and confident consumer. I also wanted to introduce you to some of the FIERCEST people I know who have impacted both my life and my career. Perhaps you know some amazing women (or men) who would consider a career in the automotive industry, and perhaps you're one of those people! I wouldn't be surprised if you were thinking, "This seems like a lot of effort and a long way around the mountain just to encourage us to sell cars." But the automotive industry unexpectedly changed my life. It has been full of incredible highs and some extremely dark valleys, but through it all, I learned what I was made of. I learned, as did Evelyn Chatel, that giving up on myself was not an option. I learned leadership and commitment, even when I felt like I was the captain on the Titanic and we had just hit the iceberg. Any time that happened, my job and responsibility were to go down with the ship after saving everyone else. After all, isn't that what a captain does?

I have worked with some of the greatest people and the greatest leaders as well as with individuals who are not worth mentioning. I believe that everything in life happens for a reason or a season. I believe that everyone has value and untapped potential. If you're in a career that you don't love, in a dead end job, are uninspired, or are simply ready to change it up, visit Cars Her Way and check out our Trusted Dealer Partners. They are always hiring great people.

I would like to personally invite you to tune in to my Facebook live show, which airs Monday through Friday at

6:45 AM CST, to get your daily dose of inspiration and connect with me.

Thank you for joining the Cars Her Way movement, which started way before #MeToo, #TimesUp, and several other extremely important social movements. As the most powerful retail influencer in the world, we as women have the power to change our circumstances. As I wrote this book, I wondered who might actually read it. Would it be someone looking for a car, looking for information on women's role in and influence over the auto industry, or looking for some entertaining and inspiring stories.

What I *am* sure of is that I would not change the thirty years during which I have been affiliated with the auto industry for the world. Through the people I have met—both customers and industry colleagues—am better for it.

This industry has taught me how to run a multi-million-dollar corporation, be resilient, be compassionate, and be inclusive, among many other benefits. So many industry experts jumped in and helped me with the content for this book. So many industry friends and clients allowed me to tell their stories and experiences. For that, I am grateful.

Thank you for taking this journey with me, and thank you for allowing me to be your trusted automotive expert. I hope this book gave you all the information that you ever need to make a great and thoughtful automotive purchase. I want to personally invite you to listen to my radio show, "Cars Her Way - Don't Go To The Dealership Alone," which airs every Sunday from 11:00-noon CST on news radio 740 KTRH Houston. Every week, I'll be bringing you wisdom and insights from automotive experts ready to answer all of your burning questions. I look forward to connecting with you live!

ACKNOWLEDGMENTS

Thank you to Sergio Marchionne, Laura Soave, Justin Byrd, Todd Stewart,Tim Kuniskis, Robb Andrews, Jason Stochivich, Jeff Falke, Brent Foreman, and the team at the Southwest Business Center in Dallas.

To the team at FIAT USA in Detroit and The FCA National Dealer Council, thank you for your support during these years. It was invaluable to me both personally and professionally.

To my team at FIAT of Austin, you will always hold a special place in my heart. You all have the hearts of champions and were in it to win it everyday.

To my tribe, the men and women who lift me up everyday, Rene Banglesdorf, Melinda Garvey, Cherie Mathews, Sharon Lechter, Rebecca Contreas, Lisa Beth Thomas, Jan Goss Gibson, Gigi Edwards Bryant, Rhone McCall, Glenn Lundy, Brian Benstock, Dan Moore, Chris Martinez, Frank Lopes, and Jim Wilkinson, I *cannot* imagine doing life without you.

To my husband of thirty years, James Copeland, thanks for always believing.

To Allix Copeland Jackson, my rockstar daughter and mini me.

To JT Copeland for always being my baby and someone I am incredibly proud of.

To my mom, Susan Colegrove, for always cheering me on and showing me how to overcome adversity like a champion.

To my dad, Bruce Colegrove, who I know is watching from heaven and saying, "Great job, kid."

To my automotive industry tribe, the board of women in automotive, I am *so* proud to serve with you, and I respect and love you all so much.

To the Big Sellers Tribe and my "15 Minutes of FIERCE" tribe, I love waking up with all of you every morning at 6:45am CST and feeding into your lives. You have no idea what you have done for me. For your support, friendship, and loyalty, I am forever grateful.

ABOUT THE AUTHOR

Lisa Copeland is an international keynote speaker, television personality, host of iHeartRadio's "Cars Her Way" talk show, bestselling author, podcast host, regular Fox Business automotive contributor, award winning sales expert, and former automotive dealer principle.

A leading expert and advocate for female consumers, Lisa works with automotive dealers and manufacturers worldwide to help them better understand the female consumer as well as create traditional and digital marketing strategies that appeal to the number one influencer in the world: women!

Her call-in show on news radio 740 KTRH Houston airs on Sundays, on which she and her co-host, Chris Martinez, help women navigate the "murky" waters of car buying.

With more than 30 years of proven success, Lisa Copeland is a dedicated pioneer in the field of automotive sales and brand strategy, having coached hundreds of businesses and spoken to sold-out audiences. In 2015, Lisa was named one of the Top 100 Women in the automotive industry and has won the Walter P. Chrysler Award for Sales and Service Excellence. Her success story has been featured in prominent publications including *The Wall Street Journal, The New York Times, Marie Claire, Fox Business,* and *Bloomberg.*

www.LisaCopeland.com

facebook.com/SpeakerLisaCopeland

twitter.com/lisaccopeland

instagram.com/real_lisacopeland

REFERENCES

1. http://girlsautoclinic.com/aboutgac/

2. https://www.mckinsey.com/industries/automotive-and-assembly/our-insights/disruptive-trends-that-will-transform-the-auto-industry

3. *https://www.marieclaire.com/career-advice/news/a18006/mary-barra-gm-ceo/*

4. https://women-drivers.com/2017-us-womens-car-dealer-report.pdf

5. https://usautosales.info/blogs/1924/the-perfect-car/front-wheel-drive-vs-rear-wheel-drive/

Made in the USA
Lexington, KY
16 June 2019